JOURNEYING
Through the Days

| *A Calendar & Journal for Personal Reflection* | 2003 |

UPPER
ROOM BOOKS®
NASHVILLE

Cover photograph: © International Robert Cushman Hayes
Cover design: Ed Maksimowicz
Interior design: Ed Maksimowicz
Interior implementation: Nancy J. Cole
First printing: 2002

ISBN 0-8358-0956-0

Printed in the United States of America

JOURNALING
BREATHING SPACE IN THE SPIRITUAL JOURNEY

I felt the pressure building as I griped at my son for breaking his lunch box. A few days before, my husband, Greg, had been laid off for the third time. Every time something broke or wore out at home, my tightly bound panic broke loose. I needed to quiet myself before I heaped more unfeeling words on my family. Feeling drawn toward my bedroom, I finished preparing lunch and slipped onto my bed—not to sleep but to pull out an untidy spiral notebook and spread my grief before God:

> God, I'm angry that Greg was laid off. He was the second-top salesman! I'm angry that I don't make more money. I'm angry that we live simply and spend money wisely, but we can't afford to buy frozen pizza. Now, without Greg's paycheck, I feel forced to make money magically appear. I know I need to trust you more, but I don't like the way circumstances are forcing me into it.

Within the rhythm of our relationship with God, there are times when praying and meditating seem too ethereal, but gripping a pen seems just right. Whatever is churning within us flows through the arm, cascades through the fingers into the pen, and splashes onto the page. There it is for God to see, for us to see.

In that quiet space of journaling, we develop a conversation with God in which we offer our self-absorbed ideas and then allow them to be swallowed up in the goals God is cultivating in us. We confess the faults and mistakes that we find so difficult to admit elsewhere. We record flashes of insight and treasured moments of encountering God.

Perhaps you have not tried journaling because it sounds like too much work. I didn't journal for many years for that reason. But when crises repeatedly erupted, I dug out that old notebook and began writing. Some folks think they have to journal every day, but that's not true. I journal as needed, which may be once a month or every day for a week. I apply the same principle to journaling that Christ applied to the sabbath: people were not created for journaling; journaling was created for people (see Mark 2:27). Keep alert for moments when you can't *avoid* journaling. When you feel the urge to confess, to grieve, to rejoice, to surrender, act on it. Pouring out such feelings before God helps you find your center in God.

MORE THAN CHRONICLING EVENTS

The spiritual discipline of journaling moves beyond and behind descriptions of life events, providing a place to ponder the pattern our lives are weaving. If a journal answers just one question, it is *What is God doing in my life?*

Some of David's psalms have the characteristics of a journal. When the Philistines seized David, he described these events in a typical journaling structure. He began by *stating what happened*: "My enemies trample on me all day long" (Psalm 56:2, NRSV). He then *recorded his feelings* of fear: "When I am afraid" (v. 3). He *expressed his (sinister) desires* to God: "Repay them for their crime" (v. 7). Concluding with what may have been David's way of *being accountable to God*, he revealed what he planned to do: "I will render thank offerings to you" (v. 12). David's rigorous honesty reveals that journaling is a place to pour out anguish, think the unthinkable, and presume to know what's best. In this safe haven, we stumble across our true motives, feelings, and desires.

This biblical pattern of reflection gives us permission to ask God questions, to try out new choices, to be less than perfect. A journal becomes the arm of God, embracing us and allowing us to look safely at feelings that overwhelm us and situations that don't make sense.

In my journal, I can confess offenses I could never admit out loud to anyone. At some point, God speaks to me about what I can do to slough off these offenses, such as praying for my neighbor. But will I do what God advises? I need to cement my commitment somewhere. I need to "put it in writing." This intangible moment needs to be recorded so as to produce a distinct wrinkle in my memory. "This, I will do (with God's grace)!"

HEARING GOD'S VOICE

Sometimes we don't know what to think about events and feelings. How can we journal then? Writing about our confusion may give us a new way of seeing. This experience is familiar to author Madeleine L'Engle:

> Not long ago someone I love said something which wounded me grievously, and I was desolate that this person could possibly have made such a comment to me.
>
> So, in great pain, I crawled to my journal and wrote it all out in a great burst of self-pity. And when I had set it down, when I had it before me, I saw that something I myself had said had called forth the words which had hurt me so. It had, in fact, been my own fault. But I would never have seen it if I had not written it out (from *Walking on Water*, p. 137).

Spirit-directed insights occur in journaling partly because we relinquish our confusion to the page in front of us. That act of relinquishment sets the stage for us to hear God's voice. After writing about what's troubling us, we may shift to other topics, only to find ourselves scribbling new perceptions and drawing arrows up to that sentence full of troubles. In those scribbled connections God speaks to us.

On the other hand, we may leave our journal filled with unanswered questions—Can I? Will I? When will God . . . ? This openness prepares us to hear fragments of answers when they emerge in the encouragement of a friend or the confrontation of a co-worker. In the meantime, we've learned to listen and to rest even when life is full of ferment.

RECORDING OUR SPIRITUAL JOURNEY

The spiritual life holds moments too choice to be forgotten: prayers that are answered; discernment that helps us deal with people; goals and dreams that remind us who we are and where we are going; moments when God's grace peeks through the clouds; those occasional miracles that no one would believe. Recording these moments affirms who we are and how God is using us. We need to celebrate these changes for which we've fought so hard. God, the only audience for our journal, is no doubt celebrating too.

Deepening understandings gained in meditation beg to be written down. We might imagine ourselves as part of a biblical story, assuming the identity of one of the characters, and then record what we discover. Try this exercise: Imagine yourself in the rich young ruler's place, requesting Jesus' advice. What would Jesus ask you to give up? Perhaps you are afraid to think what it could be. Realize that Christ looks at you and loves you before he speaks (Mark 10:21). This knowledge makes facing the truth a little easier. Ask Jesus to show you what is affecting decisions in your life.

Rereading our journals can amplify God's voice as we note trends in how God has been at work in our lives. The earliest pages of my journal are filled with statements about being unloved and undervalued. I begged for reassurance. As I look through later pages, I see those statements gradually decreasing in frequency. I find declarations that I am loved and valued by God even in my most disgusting moments. I see myself absorbing a truth that eluded me for years.

My journal is one of the many proofs that I cannot chase God away. This prodigal child can question God, rail at her enemies, or languish in self-pity, and still she's welcomed back to the journal. After weeks of absence from my journal, I am not greeted with guilt on my return. As soon as my pen touches the page, loving communication is flowing between God and me. Journaling is one more way I can enter God's rest.

Hear the invitation: "A sabbath rest still remains for the people of God. . . . Let us therefore make every effort to enter that rest" (Heb. 4:9, 11, NRSV).

—Jan Johnson

Jan Johnson is a retreat speaker and the author of Growing Compassionate Kids *and* When the Soul Listens.

[The acts] of the soul are inward but habitual,
continued, direct, living, deep, simple,
unconscious, and like a gentle and continual
bathing in the ocean of God's love. | Madame Guyon

Friday - April 11, 2003 - New Years Day can be any day.

I have been sick since
ast Saturday - even went
o doctor. Took off
ues - today as sick pay

> *Praise the LORD! Praise the LORD from the heavens; praise him in the heights! . . . Praise him, sun and moon; praise him, all you shining stars!*
> —Psalm 148:1, 3, NRSV

rian, Amanda, and John are taking the
ehicles South for the summer. The cat went
ast week & the computer today. This is
he earliest he has ever left. THIS is the
ear I do all the stuff I usually regret
ot doing every October.

p coming - Jill's surgery next week, Melissa's
aduation May 10th; UMC conference in June.
he first hot thing is speaking April 27th.

, today - Happy New Year - one step at a
me. Two boxes of rubber stamp stuff, Computer
aper supplies - not finished

turday 4/12 - briefly at church. The kids are
rving a coffee time before church tomorrow. I
ould like to see how it works. But I am
aking one more "vacation" day

e new size box of fabric
morrow - send out cards, work on Amish
rint project - finish it!

Isaiah 61:10–62:3
Psalm 98 *or* Psalm 148
Galatians 4:4-7
Luke 2:22-40

Wednesday 4/16 What are my projects?

MONDAY • DECEMBER 30

Arise, shine; for your light has come, and the glory of the LORD has risen upon you.

Isaiah 60:1, NRSV

Everything is on hold this week until Jill is settled. Things are looking good with her going home today.

I am still trying to keep up with the day-to-day stuff and the inside of my car and the windows.

Work on the back room and finish the Amish print project.

That is   two ongoing regular & car
          one long term — back room
          one short term — sewing

Thursday, Friday, Saturday— Church Services

TUESDAY • DECEMBER 31

But when the fullness of time had come, God sent his Son, born of a woman, born under the law, in order to redeem those who were under the law, so that we might receive adoption as children. . . . So you are no longer a slave but a child, and if a child then also an heir, through God.

Galatians 4:4-5, 7, NRSV

I need to fix the altar decoration.

This puts me up to five items.

Thursday 4/17 - Thank you Jill for giving me an excuse to take the day off.

monday 4/21 — the last day off

WEDNESDAY • JANUARY 1

Take Jello to the doctor
send out some cards
and enjoy last day
off.
Still pending
→ day to day stuff.
car,
back room
Amish Quilt. ←
This is about all I have energy for.
xturday 4/26 — John is home for week end
no progress

*See, darkness covers the earth and
thick darkness is over the peoples,
but the LORD rises upon you and
his glory appears over you.*
Isaiah 60:2, NIV

THURSDAY • JANUARY 2

monday 4/28 - still
behind. Sermon was
K, well received, but
never
New thing - Party for Jill   progress
pending   - day to day
car
back room
amish Quilt

*In [Christ Jesus] we have access
to God with freedom, in the
confidence born of trust in him.*
Ephesians 3:12, NEB

Tuesday April 29

FRIDAY • JANUARY 3

Federal, city, state
½ done – finish tomorrow

May the land enjoy prosperity;
may it experience righteousness.
Psalm 72:3, GNT

Party is on track – this is good.

Try for an extra hour of sleep

AND

no computer games in the Morning

Friday May 2

Day to day   Meetings next week
Car   Prayer meeting
back room
Amish quilt

SATURDAY • JANUARY 4

When they saw that the star had
stopped, they were overwhelmed
with joy. On entering the house,
they saw the child with Mary his
mother; and they knelt down and
paid him homage.
Matthew 2:10-11a, NRSV

Busy Week End

Saturday May 3

By royal decree – a free day!

But NO car. Held prayer meeting

Bath + hair – small victory.

Sunday May 4 – blew off church work.

Are you willing to believe that love is the strongest thing in the world—stronger than hate, stronger than evil, stronger than death—and that the blessed life which began in Bethlehem is the image and brightness of the Eternal Love? Then you can keep Christmas. And if you keep it for a day, why not always?

Henry Van Dyke

© International by Robert Cushman Hayes

Got some clothes ready for the week.
Two loads of laundry. Monday - Startover

Sunday May 11, 2003

made it thru graduation and party. Skipped
church + visited Grandma
at Dorothy's

Found insurance card +
paid house insurance

*This mystery . . . is that through
the gospel the Gentiles are heirs
together with Israel, members
together of one body, and
sharers together in the promise
in Christ Jesus.*
Ephesians 3:6, NIV

Skipped prayermeeting for party. Pastor
Paula was able to attend

Not making much progress on regular
stuff

1. Day to day   4. Amish quilt
2. car   5. Meetings
3. back room

Monday May 12, 2003 Let's get back
to basics. (Skipped SPPRC)

Extra hour of sleep
No computor games in the A.M.
Prepare for Worship
Prepare for Disciple

Isaiah 60:1-6
Psalm 72:1-7, 10-14
Ephesians 3:1-12
Matthew 2:1-12

Friday May 16, 2003

MONDAY • JANUARY 6

Take it one day at a time. Worship meeting went well. I have to get organized on summer worship.

Maggie quilt and I have agreed to take up the slack with the bulletin.

Saturday will be for yard work. Will be picking up some flowers for Art to plant.

I am trying to work on getting extra sleep. Mornings are easier when I have clothes ready + keep away from computer games.

This journal is about getting

The earth was formless and empty, darkness was over the surface of the deep, and the Spirit of God was hovering over the waters.

Genesis 1:2, NIV

TUESDAY • JANUARY 7

things done.

Praise the LORD you heavenly beings; praise his glory and power.

Psalm 29:1, GNT

I only have enough energy on a weekday to do ONE thing in the evening. If I am ever going to get anywhere, I have to get healthy.

Short list — new glasses
— dentist
— weight

Well, at least I should find out how much I weigh. I will at least think about it!

WEDNESDAY • JANUARY 8

Ascribe to the LORD the glory of his name; worship the LORD in holy splendor.

Psalm 29:2, NRSV

I dragged out the bed spread I have had since — ? when Brian was born?

This week end I want to make a dent in my bed room.

Shrimp Jambalaya — hey — maybe I'll cook.

Saturday — prayer meeting
Sunday — service at May Fair

THURSDAY • JANUARY 9

[John] announced to the people, "The man who will come after me is much greater than I am. I am not good enough even to bend down and untie his sandals."

Mark 1:7, GNT

FRIDAY • JANUARY 10

God said, "Let there be light,"
and there was light; and God saw
that the light was good, and he
separated light from darkness.
Genesis 1:3-4, NEB

Saturday
5/17

Bought seeds
2 tomato plants
going again tomorrow

I am going to make
up the patio pots.

Laundry

SATURDAY • JANUARY 11

The voice of the LORD is
powerful; the voice of the LORD
is full of majesty.
Psalm 29:4, KJV

I am for
the Garden
Party

Sunday - enjoy
the day

We make the decision as to whether
the events of our life will serve as
stepping stones or stumbling blocks. | Maxie Dunnam

Monday – May 26, 2003

SUNDAY • JANUARY 12

Made progress on the
garden and little else.

See what today brings.
At least I got to sleep in. Hey I did do
something – I read the Book of Acts,
I have to read Timothy, Titus, & Hebrews
or Wednesday.

> May the LORD give strength
> to his people!
> May the LORD bless his people
> with peace!
>
> Psalm 29:11, NRSV

Tuesday – May 27, 2003 – Well! I
got my reading done But I blew
off the Ad Board Meeting – I really
m a half bubble off level. A Holiday
week always does that

However, I did get a little bit done on
my car. In exchange I am getting
the engine light on.

GOOD WEEK

Genesis 1:1-5
Psalm 29
Acts 19:1-7
Mark 1:4-11

Monday July 21 2003

MONDAY • JANUARY 13

Well, that was a
fine predicament

*O LORD, thou hast searched me,
and known me.*
Psalm 139:1, KJV

I got myself into. One June 1st I
feel & broke Both ankles. Now, seven
weeks later, my right ankle has healed
and except for occasional swelling, is
almost back to normal.
Boy, am I glad there were no casts
involved.

The other ankle needed surgery.
I am still wearing a boot and there
is still an open area (which may
need a skin graft).

TUESDAY • JANUARY 14

I have been working
both at home & in
the office. This
week was the week
I wanted to try 40 hours. But I
am taking a day of vacation.

*Do you not know that your bodies
are members of Christ? Should
I therefore take the members of
Christ and make them members
of a prostitute? Never!*
1 Corinthians 6:15, NRSV

This is not the summer I was
expecting.

WEDNESDAY • JANUARY 15

Anyone united to the Lord
becomes one spirit with him.
1 Corinthians 6:17, NRSV

The garden is what got me into trouble,
I was carrying a flat of seedlings
when I fell

THURSDAY • JANUARY 16

The LORD . . . called as he had
before, "Samuel! Samuel!"
Samuel answered, "Speak, your
servant is listening."
1 Samuel 3:10, GNT

August 5, 2003 Tuesday

FRIDAY • JANUARY 17

Energy — I gotta get me some.

I am staying home today. My stomach objected to my Subway sandwich dinner.

Regular work is going fair to middlin. But I need to dig in

But, this being the summer of my feet, I have cranked productivity down (what productivity) and concentrated on my feet — now just my left foot.

SATURDAY • JANUARY 18

The right ankle is 100%. The left one is getting better from

the point of the open wound. I think this will heal up eventually. When I get back ankle is yet to be determined.

I can walk using the boot. I only need the walker when I

We have, indeed, to fashion our own desert where we
can withdraw every day, shake off our compulsions,
and dwell in the gentle healing presence of our Lord.
Without such a desert we will lose our own soul
while preaching the gospel to others. | Henri J. M. Nouwen

SUNDAY • JANUARY 19

first get started in
the morning.

I bought a car
last week. The
Camry rolled to 245,000! The
new car (Edmund) had only 31,000 miles
It is a 1998 Corolla. Both Jill &
Melissa have been after me for a long
time to get something.

I feel bad about wasting my lay
about time. I could have
done what ever but have neggitate

Maybe I am getting old! Back
to the beginning — I need energy.

I feel like over
cooked noodles!

1 Samuel 3:1-20
Psalm 139:1-6, 13-18
1 Corinthians 6:12-20
John 1:43-51

August 13, 2003

MONDAY • JANUARY 20

This is Mom & Dad's wedding anniversary — 1939 I think.

> The word of the LORD came to Jonah a second time, saying, "Get up, go to Nineveh, that great city, and proclaim to it the message that I tell you."
> Jonah 3:1-2, NRSV

...more time wasted from one view. But the ankle is getting better. I really wanted to work 40 hours this week. I was tired this morning and slept until 9:30.

Huh — wake up, Judith. Try sleeping 9, or at least 8 hours per night.

And I want cable in the bedroom!

TUESDAY • JANUARY 21

Stupid

> Trust in [God] at all times, O people; pour out your heart before him; God is a refuge for us.
> Psalm 62:8, NRSV

Just today, I should try going to bed early.

Square 1!

. . . Jesus came to Galilee, proclaiming the good news of God, and saying, "The time is fulfilled, and the kingdom of God has come near; repent, and believe in the good news."

Mark 1:14-15, NRSV

Take vitamins

This doesn't cost anything. There are plenty around here.

+ Calcium — Didn't dr cuevas say to take 1200 mg.

My salvation and my honor depend on God; he is my mighty rock, my refuge.

Psalm 62:7, NIV

I have to get back to sending out cards. I haven't done anything since June 1st

Jesus said to [Simon and Andrew], "Follow me and I will make you fish for people."

Mark 1:17, NRSV

8/13   8/14   8/15
Wed   Thu   Fri

fizzle fizzle

Bed early
vitamin
calcium

One thing God has spoken, two things have I heard: that you, O God, are strong, and that you, O LORD, are loving.

Psalm 62:11-12, NIV

OLD
LADY 61

Wherever we look, we see not
only confusion but beauty.
In snowflake, leaf or insect, we
discover structured patterns
of a delicacy and balance
that nothing manufactured
by human skill can equal. | Kallistos Ware

SUNDAY • JANUARY 26

*For God alone my soul waits
in silence, for my hope is
from [God].*
Psalm 62:5, NRSV

Energy and calm. Peacefulness.

Figure out how to work without shoes.
The new old lady orthopedic shoes are
very comfortable UNTIL my ankles swell.

← very calm, especially on an August
day.

For August, we have experienced
relative cool and ample rain

Next year — a good garden.
This year — get out and appreciate
the yard

I see my original list

1 day to day stuff
car ——— N/A
8 back room   Jonah 3:1-5, 10
                     Psalm 62:5-12
Amish Quilt   1 Corinthians 7:29-31
                     Mark 1:14-20

MONDAY • JANUARY 27

10 Church Work

11 Work Work

12 Bills + personal

13 OK — I know what goes here.
While I think about dieting + have
thought about it regularly for —
well — before Milly, before Brian,
before John. I went to weight
watchers a couple of times in
the past THREE DECADES. But I can't
remember

*Praise the LORD! I will give
thanks to the LORD with my
whole heart, in the company of
the upright, in the congregation.*
Psalm 111:1, NRSV

TUESDAY • JANUARY 28

when was the last
time since 1968 that
I was committed

*The LORD your God will raise up
a prophet from among you like
[Moses], and you shall listen
to him.*
Deuteronomy 18:15, NEB

Anyone who loves God is known by him.
1 Corinthians 8:3, NRSV

ARRGH!

I screwed up something loading Quicken. Try again tomorrow.

I am going to take Edmund out for a spin.

A man with an evil spirit . . . screamed, "What do you want with us, Jesus of Nazareth? Are you here to destroy us? I know who you are—you are God's holy messenger!"
Mark 1:23-24, GNT

August 18, 2003

All stations report.
I got some church work
finished

So much for calm. Joel ended up in jail
this weekend. I don't have the
luxury of worrying about it.

Start here —
    Bed early
    vitamins
    calcium
    B complex

> Great are the works of the LORD;
> they are pondered by all who
> delight in them.
> Psalm 111:2, NIV

> [The LORD's] work is
> honourable and glorious:
> and his righteousness
> endureth for ever.
> Psalm 111:3, KJV

We cannot understand any season of life unless we meditate on all of them. Spring, summer, fall, and winter stand in contrast, but in continuity. Through each of them we learn something of what it means to trust God, to love ourselves, and to love other people. Kathleen Fischer

Aug 23, 2003 — A pleasant, cool for August Day.

Art came over to wash windows + the kitchen floor. It is expensive in a way but it gets stuff done.

The way to become wise is to have reverence for the LORD; he gives sound judgment to all who obey his commands.
Psalm 111:10, GNT

Brian and Amanda are at the festival and I am home alone.

Laurie brought her new friend Joshua by this evening. He seems very nice. This business of Ron, Laurie, and Demetri living with Joel in Aunt Mary's house leaves something to be desired

Deuteronomy 18:15-20
Psalm 111
1 Corinthians 8:1-13
Mark 1:21-28

Aug 24, 2003

MONDAY • FEBRUARY 3

I am sitting in the parking lot at Bolles Harbor. There is a fresh breeze & the sun is temporarily hidden. There is a lot of green growth & I can't see the lake unless I get out of the car. But the breeze feels great

This is the most comfortable August I can remember

Those who wait for the LORD shall renew their strength, they shall mount up with wings like eagles, they shall run and not be weary, they shall walk and not faint.

Isaiah 40:31, NRSV

TUESDAY • FEBRUARY 4

My foot is + today. Walking without the walker or without hanging on is still a chore but it is ++++

I have to remember to take the vitamines

I can only thank God that this whole experience of ankle breaking turned out as well as it has.

He heals the brokenhearted, and binds up their wounds.

Psalm 147:3, NRSV

WEDNESDAY • FEBRUARY 5

This is going to be a busy week with Mary gone. There is only in church meeting — interviewing for a choir director.

I have to cast off here. I am to meet Jo Ann for dinner.

Very early in the morning, while it was still dark, Jesus got up, left the house and went off to a solitary place, where he prayed.

Mark 1:35, NIV

THURSDAY • FEBRUARY 6

Have you not known? Have you not heard? The LORD is the everlasting God. . . . He does not faint or grow weary; his understanding is unsearchable.

Isaiah 40:28, NRSV

Aug 26, 2003

FRIDAY • FEBRUARY 7

I had a nice chat with
Jilly over the weekend.
She is putting thought
into the pregnancy project. Alysha and
Rhonda are preggers and motherhood
is calling.

[Jesus] answered, "Let us go on to the neighboring towns, so that I may proclaim the message there also; for that is what I came out to do."
Mark 1:38, NRSV

She wants to use her schooling somewhere
besides the bank. She is so talented
and imaginative.

Speaking of talented daughters, Jill
continues to be busy with Theron.
It is

SATURDAY • FEBRUARY 8

great to see her doing
things which

How good it is to sing praises to our God, how pleasant and fitting to praise him!
Psalm 147:1, NIV

previously would have been out of
her comfort zone.

I went back to the boot. I end
up with more energy at the end
of the day. Whatever it takes

Creation is shot through with the
self-gift of God. The divine life,
the divine self-giving called grace,
is the secret dynamism at the
heart of creation. Maria Boulding

Aug 28, 2003

Stayed home today
Jill stopped by
with coffee. We
had a nice chat.
I have to work on

Have you not known? Have you not heard? Has it not been told you from the beginning? Have you not understood from the foundations of the earth? It is he who sits above the circle of the earth, and its inhabitants are like grasshoppers; who stretches out the heavens like a curtain, and spreads them like a tent to live in.
Isaiah 40:21-22, NRSV

Friday. The weekend is supposed to be
great, although I have church work to
do.

Well, the chore of the day.
There must be an easier
way to take a bath

Friday - stop at church to sign checks, work
tuesday - piano tuner ; check order
sunday - poll punches
monday -

Isaiah 40:21-31
Psalm 147:1-11, 20c
1 Corinthians 9:16-23
Mark 1:29-39

September 7, 2003

Not many days go down
as totally unique

But today—

Church — greeter for the first time in ages.

Picnic — stayed long enough to be polite — very tiring.

Home — wait for Milly — go to Alysha's baby shower

Call from Joel — Grandma Cline has died in her sleep

Sing praise to the LORD, all his faithful people! Remember what the Holy One has done, and give him thanks!

Psalm 30:4, GNT

Went to shower.

I was unsure at that point what to do.

I expected that it would be a strange + strained situation

[Naaman] went down and dipped himself in the Jordan seven times, as the man of God had told him, and his flesh was restored and became clean like that of a young boy.

2 Kings 5:14, NIV

WEDNESDAY • FEBRUARY 12

Received call from
Joel that it would
for me
be appropriate to be there

OK.
The bottom line was that she had
arranged for immediate cremation and
this was the only time I could see her.

When I got there, I was welcomed by
Linda, David, Richard, Lindee,
Becky & daughters were there, along with
Joel.

> [God's] anger lasts only a
> moment, his goodness for
> a lifetime.
> Psalm 30:5, GNT

THURSDAY • FEBRUARY 13

Grandma lay as
she died.

Becky & one of Cindy's
daughters, tidied up, arranged Grandma
in a more suitable position.

> Surely you know that many
> runners take part in a race, but
> only one of them wins the prize.
> Run, then, in such a way as to
> win the prize.
> 1 Corinthians 9:24, GNT

FRIDAY • FEBRUARY 14

others arrived. Most
of Richards kids
(Danny lives in Lansing).
Jill & Sharon, Brian & Melissa,
Laurie, Jimmy.

@ 20 people from the Kingdom
hall were in and out, of whom
I only know Mimi, Allen &
Buddy Halley

*Tears may linger at nightfall,
but joy comes in the morning.*
Psalm 30:5, NEB

SATURDAY • FEBRUARY 15

Actually it was neat
Nothing fake or
artificial, just
family + friends
coming together, — I hardly
recognized Kim + would never have
recognized Rick.

*A leper came to him begging him,
and kneeling he said to him,
"If you choose, you can make me
clean." Moved with pity, Jesus
stretched out his hand and
touched him, and said to him,
"I do choose. Be made clean!"*
Mark 1:40-41, NRSV

God is making room in my heart for compassion: the awareness that where my life begins is where your life begins; the awareness that the sensitiveness to your needs cannot be separated from the sensitiveness to my needs; the awareness that the joys of my heart are never mine alone—nor are my sorrows.

Howard Thurman

SUNDAY • FEBRUARY 16

We shared Grandma stories

You have changed my sadness into a joyful dance; you have taken away my sorrow and surrounded me with joy.
Psalm 30:11, GNT

Becky seemed to be quietly in charge with even Richard deferring to her.

After the paramedics, the coroner, her doctor, and the police passed in the event, we alerted the funeral home. They would come when we were ready.

Family were in & out. Jessica came, JoAnn, and finally Aunt Mary.

Both she and David seemed accepting of the event.

Mary was aware of every one. She looks very frail.

2 Kings 5:1-14
Psalm 30
1 Corinthians 9:24-27
Mark 1:40-45

September 8, 2003

MONDAY • FEBRUARY 17

The house was warm & just a little stuffy. Joel said that he, Richard & Linda, Becky & a daughter & grandson closed the place. Richard NEVER took off his suit jacket.

I am helping Joel to get in touch with Gilbert.

There will be a memorial service next Sunday

I will make for you a covenant on that day with the wild animals, the birds of the air, and the creeping things of the ground; and I will abolish the bow, the sword, and war from the land; and I will make you lie down in safety.

Hosea 2:18, NRSV

TUESDAY • FEBRUARY 18

There is a big potential for "weird" there.

I feel settled about Ma. I have known for years how she felt about me. She told me that she has daughters-in-law but only one daughter — me

Happy are those who are concerned for the poor; the LORD will help them when they are in trouble.

Psalm 41:1, GNT

WEDNESDAY • FEBRUARY 19

In [Jesus Christ] every one of God's promises is a "Yes."
2 Corinthians 1:20, NRSV

Her life has been difficult over time But she has been a loving mother to me and is the universal grand mother

She knows now what the "truth" is.

Joel will read this and understand the inuendo.

This was another life and literally decades ago.

THURSDAY • FEBRUARY 20

[Jesus] said to the paralytic, "I tell you, get up, take your mat and go home."
Mark 2:10-11, NIV

Gilbert — Show me the money
½ of house — david pay rent.
Gilbert — one of the constants in the universe

I think that this is the last straw for Joel.

FRIDAY • FEBRUARY 21

Georg is coming. I had a chat with Holly

God said, "I, even I, am he who blots out your transgressions, for my own sake, and remembers your sin no more."
Isaiah 43:25, NIV

I have enjoyed my day off. I am getting really lazy.

SATURDAY • FEBRUARY 22

You have upheld me because of my integrity, and set me in your presence forever.
Psalm 41:12, NRSV

Now that [Jesus] has come, we know God stands with us in every season of our lives. We know because Jesus lived life just as you and I do. He was not a celestial visitor who just dropped in for a casual visit. He was a human being who worked long and hard, faced temptation, knew joy and sorrow. | Kenneth L. Gibble

September 15, 2003.

This coming Sunday I will be able to attend the Disciple 2 class. I am going to more conscious about studying for the class.

There is so much to do in so many areas of my life.

Lists only make me a slave to the list.

I have a Finance meeting tomorrow which I can handle using the report I did earlier.

Do not remember the former things, or consider the things of old. I am about to do a new thing; now it springs forth, do you not perceive it? I will make a way in the wilderness and rivers in the desert.

Isaiah 43:18-19, NRSV

Isn't this beautiful

Isaiah 43:18-25
Psalm 41
2 Corinthians 1:18-22
Mark 2:1-12

September 16, 2003 Tuesday

Finance meeting; low attendance; I learned more than I need to know about the nay sayers.

This is a big hurdle to overcome. People are unhappy with the D.S, unhappy with the pastor, unhappy

The Mighty One, God, the LORD, speaks and summons the earth from the rising of the sun to the place where it sets.

Psalm 50:1, NIV

TUESDAY • FEBRUARY 25

Our God comes and does not keep silence, before him is a devouring fire, and a mighty tempest all around him.

Psalm 50:3, NRSV

September 30, 2003, Tuesday

WEDNESDAY • FEBRUARY 26

*It is not ourselves that we preach;
we preach Jesus Christ as Lord.*

2 Corinthians 4:5, GNT

Sun Disciple
Mon —————
Tue Lay Leadership
Wed Wed night
Thu S/PPRC
Fri V.J.
Sat Breathe

THURSDAY • FEBRUARY 27

*Whey they had crossed [the dry
riverbed of the Jordan], Elijah
said to Elisha, "Tell me what I
may do for you, before I am taken
from you." Elisha said, "Please
let me inherit a double share of
your spirit."*

2 Kings 2:9, NRSV

Tuesday ~ October 7, 2003

Sun – Disciple X
Mon ————
Tues – Cumc Aumc
          meeting
Wed – evening program
Thu – ??
Friday
Saturday

As [Elijah and Elisha] continued walking and talking, a chariot of fire and horses of fire separated the two of them, and Elijah ascended in a whirlwind into heaven.

2 Kings 2:11, NRSV

Breathe
Trying to sleep in bed.
Trying to adjust back
to John being home. I have 14 days.

It is the God who said, "Let light shine out of darkness," who has shone in our hearts to give the light of the knowledge of the glory of God in the face of Jesus Christ.

2 Corinthians 4:6, NRSV

Ye are the light of the world—but only because
you are enkindled, made radiant by the One
Light of the World. And being kindled, we have
got to get on with it, be useful. | Evelyn Underhill

*[Jesus] was transfigured before
[Peter, James, and John], and
his clothes became dazzling
white. . . . Then a cloud
overshadowed them, . . . and
there came a voice, "This is my
Son, the Beloved; listen to him!"*
Mark 9:2b-3, 7, NRSV

2 Kings 2:1-12
Psalm 50:1-6
2 Corinthians 4:3-6
Mark 9:2-9

Do not remember the sins of
my youth or my transgressions;
according to your steadfast love
remember me, for your goodness'
sake, O LORD!

Psalm 25:7, NRSV

Then God said to Noah and to
his sons with him, "As for me, I
am establishing my covenant with
you and your descendants after
you, and with every living
creature that is with you."

Genesis 9:8-10a, NRSV

ASH WEDNESDAY

*For Christ also suffered for
sins once for all, the righteous
for the unrighteous, in order to
bring you to God. He was put to
death in the flesh, but made alive
in the spirit.*

1 Peter 3:18, NRSV

*Make me know your ways,
O LORD; teach me your paths.*

Psalm 25:4, NRSV

FRIDAY • MARCH 7

*[Jesus] was in the wilderness
forty days, tempted by Satan;
and he was with the wild beasts;
and the angels waited on him.*

Mark 1:12, NRSV

SATURDAY • MARCH 8

*And baptism . . . now saves
you—not as a removal of dirt
from the body, but as an appeal
to God for a good conscience,
through the resurrection of
Jesus Christ.*

1 Peter 3:21, NRSV

Not knowing where we are going forces us to pay attention to where we are. Since we don't know where *there* is, we have to content ourselves with *here*, now, this moment, this spot, this tree, this sound, this breeze, this twist in the road. Renita J. Weems

In those days Jesus came from Nazareth of Galilee and was baptized by John in the Jordan. And just as he was coming up out of the water, he saw the heavens torn apart and the Spirit descending like a dove on him.

Mark 1:9-10, NRSV

Genesis 9:8-17
Psalm 25:1-10
1 Peter 3:18-22
Mark 1:9-15

*The promise that he would
inherit the world did not come to
Abraham or to his descendants
through the law but through the
righteousness of faith.*

Romans 4:13, NRSV

*[The LORD] does not neglect the
poor or ignore their suffering;
he does not turn away from
them, but answers when they
call for help.*

Psalm 22:24, GNT

[Jesus] . . . said, "If any want to become my followers, let them deny themselves and take up their cross and follow me."

Mark 8:34, NRSV

Let all the ends of the earth remember and turn again to the LORD; let all the families of the nations bow down before him.

Psalm 22:27, NEB

What will it profit them to gain the whole world and forfeit their life?

Mark 8:36, NRSV

Future generations will be told about the LORD, and proclaim his deliverance to a people yet unborn.

Psalm 22:30-31, NRSV

Keep yourself as a pilgrim and a stranger here in this world, as one to whom the world's business counts but little. Keep your heart free, and always lift it up to God, for you have here no city long abiding. Send your desires and your prayers always up to God. Thomas à Kempis

SECOND SUNDAY IN LENT

[Abraham] grew strong in his faith as he gave glory to God, being fully convinced that God was able to do what he had promised. Therefore his faith "was reckoned to him as righteousness."

Romans 4:20-22, NRSV

Genesis 17:1-7, 15-16
Psalm 22:23-31
Romans 4:13-25
Mark 8:31-38

The message about Christ's death on the cross is nonsense to those who are being lost; but for us who are being saved it is God's power.

1 Corinthians 1:18, GNT

Making a whip of cords, [Jesus] drove all of them out of the temple, both the sheep and the cattle. He also poured out the coins of the money changers and overturned their tables.

John 2:15, NRSV

God said, "I am the LORD your God. . . . You shall have no other gods before me."
Exodus 20:2-3, NIV

We proclaim Christ crucified, a stumbling block to Jews and foolishness to Gentiles, but to those who are the called, both Jews and Greeks, Christ the power of God and the wisdom of God.
1 Corinthians 1:23-24, NRSV

*What seems to be God's
foolishness is wiser than human
wisdom, and what seems to be
God's weakness is stronger than
human strength.*

1 Corinthians 1:25, GNT

*The law of the LORD is perfect,
converting the soul; the testimony
of the LORD is sure, making wise
the simple.*

Psalm 19:7, KJV

Our hearts and flesh cry out for the living God, Who
IS here, right now, among us if we but receive that
Divine Presence. The call to "take time to be holy" is a
call to integrate prayer and life, for they are, in fact,
one. The call is to live as if all time were Sabbath time.

Bonnie Thurston

THIRD SUNDAY IN LENT

Remember the Sabbath day by keeping it holy. Six days you shall labor and do all your work, but the seventh day is a Sabbath to the LORD your God.

Exodus 20:8-10, NIV

Exodus 20:1-17
Psalm 19
1 Corinthians 1:18-25
John 2:13-22

*Then they cried to the LORD in
their trouble, and he saved them
from their distress; he sent out his
word and healed them.*

Psalm 107:19-20a, NRSV

*God has made us what we are,
and in our union with Christ
Jesus he has created us for a
life of good deeds, which he has
already prepared for us to do.*

Ephesians 2:10, GNT

*This is the judgment, that the
light has come into the world, and
people loved darkness rather than
light because their deeds were evil.*

John 3:19, NRSV

*God so loved the world that he
gave his one and only Son, that
whoever believes in him shall not
perish but have eternal life.*

John 3:16, NIV

*It was not to judge the world that
God sent his Son into the world,
but that through him the world
might be saved.*

John 3:17, NEB

*Those who do what is true come
to the light, so that it may be
clearly seen that their deeds
have been done in God.*

John 3:21, NRSV

The real monastic walks
through life with a barefooted
soul, alert, aware, grateful, and
only partially at home. | Joan Chittister

FOURTH SUNDAY IN LENT

*God's mercy is so abundant,
and his love for us is so great,
that while we were spiritually
dead in our disobedience he
brought us to life with Christ.*

Ephesians 2:4-5, GNT

Numbers 21:4-9
Psalm 107:1-3, 17-22
Ephesians 2:1-10
John 3:14-21

MONDAY • MARCH 31

Have mercy upon me, O God,
according to thy lovingkindness:
according unto the multitude of
thy tender mercies blot out my
transgressions.

Psalm 51:1, KJV

TUESDAY • APRIL 1

Having been made perfect, [Jesus]
became the source of eternal
salvation for all who obey him.

Hebrews 5:9, NRSV

. . . they shall all know me, from the least of them to the greatest, says the LORD; *for I will forgive their iniquity, and remember their sin no more.*

Jeremiah 31:34, NRSV

Jesus said, "Whoever serves me must follow me; and where I am, my servant also will be."

John 12:26, NIV

Those who love their life lose it, and those who hate their life in this world will keep it for eternal life.

John 12:25, NRSV

Create a pure heart in me, O God, and put a new and loyal spirit in me.

Psalm 51:10, GNT

Here we have the mystery that to recover the lost coin within ourselves—our own unredeemed humanity—is to recover Christ the King himself. . . . He is hidden in the depths of the unconscious, where he is both the savior and the one to be saved. He comes in dirt and mire and in all that is objectionable, but when he is recovered to consciousness, we gaze upon ineffable beauty! | John Sanford

FIFTH SUNDAY IN LENT

Jesus said, "Now my soul is troubled. And what should I say—'Father, save me from this hour'? No, it is for this reason that I have come to this hour. Father, glorify your name."
John 12:27-28, NRSV

Jeremiah 31:31-34
Psalm 51:1-12
Hebrews 5:5-10
John 12:20-33

MONDAY • APRIL 7

I trusted in thee, O LORD:
I said, thou art my God. My
times are in thy hand.
Psalm 31:14-15, KJV

TUESDAY • APRIL 8

The Sovereign LORD has taught
me what to say, so that I can
strengthen the weary. Every
morning he makes me eager to
hear what he is going to teach me.
Isaiah 50:4, GNT

WEDNESDAY • APRIL 9

*God . . . highly exalted him and
gave him the name that is above
every name, so that at the name
of Jesus . . . every tongue should
confess that Jesus Christ is Lord.*

Philippians 2:9-11, NRSV

THURSDAY • APRIL 10

*The Sovereign LORD himself
defends me—
    who, then, can prove me guilty?*

Isaiah 50:9, GNT

FRIDAY • APRIL 11

"Abba, Father," [Jesus] said,
"everything is possible for you.
Take this cup from me. Yet not
what I will, but what you will."
Mark 14:36, NIV

SATURDAY • APRIL 12

Let your face shine on your
servant; save me in your
unfailing love.
Psalm 31:16, NIV

By the Passion we are able to see
ourselves in a new light. By the
suffering of Jesus we can be
agents of change, knowing that
we are accepted and forgiven.
This is available to all. Kevin Scully

PASSION/PALM SUNDAY

Let the same mind be in you that was in Christ Jesus, who, though he was in the form of God, did not regard equality with God as something to be exploited, but . . . humbled himself and became obedient to the point of death.

Philippians 2:5-8, NRSV

Isaiah 50:4-9*a*
Psalm 31:9-16
Philippians 2:5-11
Mark 14:1–15:47
 or Mark 15:1-39 (40-47)

The stone that the builders
rejected has become the chief
cornerstone.

Psalm 118:22, NRSV

Peter said, *"I truly understand*
that God shows no partiality, but
in every nation anyone who fears
him and does what is right is
acceptable to him."

Acts 10:34-35, NRSV

Give thanks to the LORD, for he is good; his love endures forever.

Psalm 118:1, NIV

MAUNDY THURSDAY

As often as you eat this bread and drink the cup, you proclaim the Lord's death until he comes.

1 Corinthians 11:26, NRSV

FRIDAY • APRIL 18

GOOD FRIDAY

*I will not die; instead I will
live and proclaim what the LORD
has done.*

Psalm 118:17, GNT

SATURDAY • APRIL 19

*That message [peace by Jesus
Christ] spread throughout
Judea . . . how God anointed
Jesus of Nazareth with the Holy
Spirit and with power; how he
went about doing good and
healing all who were oppressed by
the devil, for God was with him.*

Acts 10:37-38, NRSV

Death is natural. Loss is natural. Grief is natural. But those stones have been rolled away this happy morning, to reveal the highly unnatural truth. By the light of this day, God has planted a seed of life in us that cannot be killed, and if we can remember that then there is nothing we cannot do: move mountains, banish fear, love our enemies, change the world. Barbara Brown Taylor

EASTER SUNDAY

*Early on the first day of the week,
while it was still dark, Mary
Magdalene came to the tomb and
saw that the stone had been
removed from the tomb.*

John 20:1, NRSV

Acts 10:34-43
Psalm 118:1-2, 14-24
1 Corinthians 11:23-26; 15:1-11
Mark 16:1-8 *or* John 20:1-18

MONDAY • APRIL 21

*. . . God is light and in him there
is no darkness at all.*
1 John 1:5, NRSV

TUESDAY • APRIL 22

*How very good and pleasant it
is when kindred live together
in unity!*
Psalm 133:1, NRSV

*Jesus did many other miraculous
signs in the presence of his
disciples, which are not recorded
in this book. But these are written
that you may believe that Jesus is
the Christ, the Son of God, and
that by believing you may have
life in his name.*

John 20:30-31, NIV

*The whole group of those who
believed were of one heart and
soul, and no one claimed private
ownership of any possessions, but
everything they owned was held
in common.*

Acts 4:32, NRSV

There was not a needy person among [those who believed], for as many as owned lands or houses sold them and brought the proceeds . . . and it was distributed to each as any had need.

Acts 4:34-35, NRSV

Jesus said, "Peace be with you! As the Father has sent me, I am sending you." And with that he breathed on them and said, "Receive the Holy Spirit."

John 20:21-22, NIV

God has called us into being as a community and
our life as a community, though fraught with
struggles and failures, is a powerful act of
revelation, testimony, and service.

Rule of the Society of
St. John the Evangelist

If anyone does sin, we have someone who pleads with the Father on our behalf—Jesus Christ, the righteous one. And Christ himself is the means by which our sins are forgiven, and not our sins only, but also the sins of everyone.

1 John 2:1-2, GNT

Acts 4:32-35
Psalm 133
1 John 1:1–2:2
John 20:19-31

See what love the Father has given us, that we should be called children of God; and that is what we are.

1 John 3:1, NRSV

What you see and know was done by faith in [Jesus'] name; it was faith in Jesus that has made [the lame man] well.

Acts 3:16a, GNT

*[Jesus] said to [the disciples],
"Why are you troubled, and why
do doubts rise in your minds?
Look at my hands and feet. It
is I myself!"*

Luke 24:38-39, NIV

*When you are disturbed, do not
sin; ponder it on your beds, and
be silent.*

Psalm 4:4, NRSV

*Let no one deceive you, my
children! Whoever does what is
right is righteous, just as Christ
is righteous.*

1 John 3:7, GNT

*I will both lay me down in peace,
and sleep: for thou, LORD, only
makest me dwell in safety.*

Psalm 4:8, KJV

. . . live as a child of God, and you will be able to
pray and most assuredly be heard as a child. Andrew Murray

© International by Robert Cushman Hayes

Beloved, we are God's children now; what we will be has not yet been revealed. What we do know is this: when [God] is revealed, we will be like him, for we will see him as he is.

1 John 3:2, NRSV

Acts 3:12-19
Psalm 4
1 John 3:1-7
Luke 24:36b-48

MONDAY • MAY 5

Jesus said, *"I am the good shepherd. The good shepherd lays down his life for the sheep."*

John 10:11, NRSV

TUESDAY • MAY 6

Surely goodness and love will follow me all the days of my life, and I will dwell in the house of the LORD forever.

Psalm 23:6, NIV

*And this is [God's]
commandment, that we should
believe in the name of his Son
Jesus Christ and love one another,
just as he has commanded us.*
1 John 3:23, NRSV

*How does God's love abide in
anyone who has the world's goods
and sees a brother or sister in
need and yet refuses help?*
1 John 3:17, NRSV

This is how we know what love is:
Christ gave his life for us. We
too, then, ought to give our lives
for others!

1 John 3:16, GNT

He leads me beside still waters;
he restores my soul. . . . Even
though I walk through the darkest
valley, I fear no evil; for you are
with me; your rod and your
staff—they comfort me.

Psalm 23:2b-4, NRSV

Because Christ is risen, we need
no longer be afraid of any dark
or evil force in the universe. | Kallistos Ware

*Dear children, let us not love
with words or tongue but with
actions and in truth.*

1 John 3:18, NIV

Acts 4:5-12
Psalm 23
1 John 3:16-24
John 10:11-18

Jesus said, *"I am the true vine and my Father is the gardener. He cuts off every branch in me that bears no fruit, while every branch that does bear fruit he trims clean so that it will be even more fruitful."*

John 15:1-2, NIV

All the ends of the earth shall remember and turn to the LORD; and all the families of the nations shall worship before him.

Psalm 22:27, NRSV

*Beloved, let us love one another,
because love is from God.*

1 John 4:7, NRSV

*This is how God showed his love
among us: He sent his one and
only Son into the world that we
might live through him.*

1 John 4:9, NIV

*No one has ever seen God, but
if we love one another, God lives
in union with us, and his love is
made perfect in us.*

1 John 4:12, GNT

*The commandment we have from
[Jesus] is this: those who love
God must love their brothers
and sisters also.*

1 John 4:21, NRSV

. . . the essential thing is to get
within you the growing life,
and then you cannot help but
grow. . . . Abide in the Vine.

Hannah Whitall Smith

Jesus said, *"I am the vine, you are the branches. Those who abide in me and I in them bear much fruit, because apart from me you can do nothing."*

John 15:5, NRSV

Acts 8:26-40
Psalm 22:25-31
1 John 4:7-21
John 15:1-8

Jesus said, *"If you obey my commands, you will remain in my love, just as I have obeyed my Father's commands and remain in his love."*

John 15:10, GNT

Make a joyful noise to the LORD, all the earth; break forth into joyous song and sing praises.

Psalm 98:4, NRSV

WEDNESDAY • MAY 21

*Let the floods clap their hands: let
the hills be joyful together before
the LORD; for he cometh to judge
the earth: with righteousness shall
he judge the world, and the people
with equity.*

Psalm 98:8-9, KJV

THURSDAY • MAY 22

*This is how we know that we love
the children of God: by loving
God and carrying out his
commands.*

1 John 5:2, NIV

*Peter said, "Can anyone keep
these people from being baptized
with water? They have received
the Holy Spirit just as we have."*

Acts 10:47, NIV

*Let the sea roar, and all that fills
it; the world and those who live
in it. Let the floods clap their
hands; let the hills sing together
for joy at the presence of the
LORD.*

Psalm 98:7-8a, NRSV

I asked the earth; and it answered, "I am not He;" and whatsoever are therein made the same confession. I asked the sea and the deeps, and the creeping things that lived, and they replied, "We are not thy God, seek higher than we."   Saint Augustine

*Jesus said, "You did not choose
me but I chose you. And I
appointed you to go and bear
fruit, fruit that will last, so that
the Father will give you whatever
you ask him in my name."*
John 15:16, NRSV

Acts 10:44-48
Psalm 98
1 John 5:1-6
John 15:9-17

*Jesus prayed, "I have made
your name known to those
whom you gave me from the
world. They were yours, and
you gave them to me, and they
have kept your word."*

John 17:6, NRSV

*[The person who does not walk in
the counsel of the wicked] is like a
tree planted by streams of water,
which yields its fruit in season
and whose leaf does not wither.*

Psalm 1:3, NIV

WEDNESDAY • MAY 28

The testimony is this: God has given us eternal life, and this life has its source in his Son.

1 John 5:11, GNT

THURSDAY • MAY 29

Jesus prayed, "And now I am no longer in the world, but [my disciples] are in the world, and I am coming to you. Holy Father, protect them in your name that you have given me, so that they may be one, as we are one."

John 17:11, NRSV

FRIDAY • MAY 30

The LORD knoweth the way of the righteous: but the way of the ungodly shall perish.

Psalm 1:6, KJV

SATURDAY • MAY 31

Anyone who believes in the Son of God has [God's] testimony (about the Son) in his heart.

1 John 5:10, NIV

. . . be great believers! Little faith will bring your souls to Heaven, but great faith will bring Heaven to your souls. Charles H. Spurgeon

Jesus said, *"I have given them your word, and the world has hated them because they do not belong to the world, just as I do not belong to the world. I am not asking you to take them out of the world, but I ask you to protect them from the evil one."*

John 17:14-15, NRSV

Acts 1:15-17, 21-26
Psalm 1
1 John 5:9-13
John 17:6-19

MONDAY • JUNE 2

How many are your works,
O LORD! In wisdom you made
them all; the earth is full of
your creatures.

Psalm 104:24, NIV

TUESDAY • JUNE 3

We know that the whole creation
has been groaning in labor pains
until now; and not only the
creation, but we ourselves, who
have the first fruits of the Spirit,
groan inwardly while we wait
for adoption, the redemption of
our bodies.

Romans 8:22-23, NRSV

Jesus said, "It is to your advantage that I go away, for if I do not go away, the Advocate will not come to you; but if I go, I will send him to you."

John 16:7, NRSV

It was by hope that we were saved; but if we see what we hope for, then it is not really hope. . . . But if we hope for what we do not see, we wait for it with patience.

Romans 8:24-25, GNT

FRIDAY • JUNE 6

We do not know how we ought to pray; the Spirit himself pleads with God for us in groans that words cannot express.

Romans 8:26, GNT

SATURDAY • JUNE 7

May the glory of the LORD stand for ever and may he rejoice in his works!

Psalm 104:31, NEB

In proportion to the depth and the breadth of any and every creature's nature, the creature possesses, or can attain to, the consciousness that God is its sole ultimate rest, sole pure delight.

Baron Friedrich
von Hügel

PENTECOST

*Suddenly from heaven there came
a sound like the rush of a violent
wind, and it filled the entire
house where they were sitting.
Divided tongues, as of fire,
appeared among them, and a
tongue rested on each of them.*

Acts 2:2-3, NRSV

Acts 2:1-21
Psalm 104:24-34, 35*b*
Romans 8:22-27
John 15:26-27; 16:4*b*-15

*[Isaiah] heard the voice of the
LORD saying, "Whom shall I
send? And who will go for us?"
And [Isaiah] said, "Here am I.
Send me!"*

Isaiah 6:8, NIV

*"I am telling you the truth,"
replied Jesus, "that no one can
enter the Kingdom of God unless
he is born of water and the
Spirit. . . . I tell you that you
must all be born again."*

John 3:5, 7, GNT

W E D N E S D A Y   •   J U N E 11

*The Spirit that God has given
you does not make you slaves and
cause you to be afraid; instead,
the Spirit makes you God's
children, and by the Spirit's
power we cry out to God,
"Father! my Father!"*

Romans 8:15, GNT

T H U R S D A Y   •   J U N E 12

*If [we are] children [of God],
then heirs, heirs of God and joint
heirs with Christ—if, in fact, we
suffer with him so that we may
also be glorified with him.*

Romans 8:17, NRSV

FRIDAY • JUNE 13

*A person is born physically of
human parents, but he is born
spiritually of the Spirit.*

John 3:6, GNT

SATURDAY • JUNE 14

*Jesus answered Nicodemus, "You
do not believe me when I tell you
about the things of this world;
how will you ever believe me,
then, when I tell you about the
things of heaven?"*

John 3:12, GNT

Be slow to pray. This is not an enterprise to be entered into lightly. When we pray we are using words that bring us into proximity with words that break cedars, shake the wilderness, make the oaks whirl, and strip forests bare (Psalm 29:5-9). | Eugene H. Peterson

*The voice of the LORD is
powerful; the voice of the LORD
is full of majesty. The voice
of the LORD breaks the cedars;
the LORD breaks the cedars of
Lebanon. . . . The voice of the
LORD shakes the wilderness.*

Psalm 29:4-5, 8a, NRSV

Isaiah 6:1-8
Psalm 29
Romans 8:12-17
John 3:1-17

*As servants of God we have
commended ourselves in every
way: . . . as having nothing, and
yet possessing everything.*

2 Corinthians 6:4, 10, NRSV

*Jesus stood up and commanded
the wind, "Be quiet!" and he said
to the waves, "Be still!" The
wind died down, and there was
a great calm.*

Mark 4:39, GNT

[Jesus] said to his disciples,
"Why are you so afraid? Do you
still have no faith?"

Mark 4:40, NIV

David said, *"The LORD who*
delivered me from the paw of the
lion and the paw of the bear will
deliver me from the hand of this
Philistine."

1 Samuel 17:37, NIV

Those who know your name put their trust in you, for you, O LORD, have not forsaken those who seek you.

Psalm 9:10, NRSV

[Jesus' disciples] were terribly afraid and began to say to one another, "Who is this man? Even the wind and the waves obey him!"

Mark 4:41, GNT

For, just as all the streamlets that flow
from a clear spring are as clear as the
spring itself, so the works of a soul in
grace are pleasing in the eyes both of
God and of [people], since they
proceed from this spring of life, in
which the soul is as a tree planted.   Saint Teresa of Avila

The LORD is a refuge for the oppressed, a stronghold in times of trouble.

Psalm 9:9, NIV

1 Samuel 17:1*a*, 4-11, 19-23, 32-49
Psalm 9:9-20
2 Corinthians 6:1-13
Mark 4:35-41

MONDAY • JUNE 23

From the depths of my despair
I call to you, LORD. Hear my
cry, O LORD; listen to my call
for help!
Psalm 130:1-2, GNT

TUESDAY • JUNE 24

Just as you excel in everything—
in faith, in speech, in knowledge,
in complete earnestness . . . see
that you also excel in this grace
of giving.
2 Corinthians 8:7, NIV

It is appropriate for you who began last year not only to do something but even to desire to do something—now finish doing it, so that your eagerness may be matched by completing it according to your means.

2 Corinthians 8:10-11, NRSV

If you kept a record of our sins, who could escape being condemned? But you forgive us, so that we should reverently obey you.

Psalm 130:3-4, GNT

FRIDAY • JUNE 27

Jesus said to the woman,
*"Daughter, your faith has healed
you. Go in peace and be freed
from your suffering."*
Mark 5:34, NIV

SATURDAY • JUNE 28

*Jesus said to the leader of the
synagogue, "Do not fear, only
believe."*
Mark 5:36, NRSV

Small miracles are all around us. We can find them everywhere—in our homes, in our daily activities, and, hardest to see, in ourselves. Sue Bender

*I wait for the LORD, my soul
waits, and in his word I hope;
my soul waits for the LORD
more than those who watch for
the morning.*

Psalm 130:5-6, NRSV

2 Samuel 1:1, 17-27
Psalm 130
2 Corinthians 8:7-15
Mark 5:21-43

MONDAY • JUNE 30

This God is our God for ever and ever: he will be our guide even unto death.

Psalm 48:14, KJV

TUESDAY • JULY 1

Paul wrote, *"I am content with weaknesses, insults, hardships, persecutions, and difficulties for Christ's sake. For when I am weak, then I am strong."*

2 Corinthians 12:10, GNT

[Jesus] could not do any miracles
[in his home town], except lay his
hands on a few sick people and
heal them.

Mark 6:5, NIV

Great is the LORD, and most
worthy of praise, in the city of
our God, his holy mountain.

Psalm 48:1, NIV

FRIDAY • JULY 4

[The Lord] said to [Paul],
"My grace is sufficient for
you, for power is made perfect
in weakness."

2 Corinthians 12:9, NRSV

SATURDAY • JULY 5

We ponder your steadfast love, O
God, in the midst of your temple.

Psalm 48:9, NRSV

We see that it is not the task of Christianity
to provide easy answers to every question,
but to make us progressively aware of a
mystery. God is not so much the object of
our knowledge as the cause of our wonder. | Kallistos Ware

Jesus said to the Twelve, *"If any place will not welcome you and they refuse to hear you, as you leave, shake off the dust that is on your feet as a testimony against them."*

Mark 6:11, NRSV

2 Samuel 5:1-5, 9-10
Psalm 48
2 Corinthians 12:2-10
Mark 6:1-13

*The earth is the LORD's and all
that is in it, the world and those
who dwell therein.*

Psalm 24:1, NEB

*Let us praise God for his glorious
grace, for the free gift he gave us
in his dear Son!*

Ephesians 1:6, GNT

*Who may go up the mountain of
the Lord? And who may stand
in his holy place? He who has
clean hands and a pure heart . . .*

Psalm 24:3-4, NEB

*[God] chose us in Christ before
the foundation of the world to
be holy and blameless before him
in love.*

Ephesians 1:4, NRSV

*Lift up your heads, O ye gates;
and be ye lift up, ye everlasting
doors; and the King of glory shall
come in.*

Psalm 24:7, KJV

*David and all the house of Israel
were dancing before the LORD
with all their might, with songs
and lyres and harps and
tambourines and castanets
and cymbals.*

2 Samuel 6:5, NRSV

With the gifts of love and tenderness and of the compassion of God, of Jesus Christ, we can seal the heart of another to ours as ours is sealed to God. And so begins a chain of hearts which are sealed to God and to one another.

Catherine de Hueck Doherty

[God] destined us for adoption as his children through Jesus Christ, according to the good pleasure of his will.

Ephesians 1:5, NRSV

2 Samuel 6:1-5, 12*b*-19
Psalm 24
Ephesians 1:3-14
Mark 6:14-29

MONDAY • JULY 14

You are no longer strangers and
aliens, but you are . . . members
of the household of God . . .
with Christ Jesus himself as the
cornerstone. In him the whole
structure is joined together
and grows into a holy temple
in the Lord.

Ephesians 2:19-21, NRSV

TUESDAY • JULY 15

[Christ] is our peace; in his flesh
he has made both groups into
one and has broken down the
dividing wall, that is, the
hostility between us.

Ephesians 2:14, NRSV

WEDNESDAY • JULY 16

*When Jesus got out of the boat,
he saw this large crowd, and his
heart was filled with pity for
them, because they were like sheep
without a shepherd. So he began
to teach them many things.*

Mark 6:34, GNT

THURSDAY • JULY 17

*[Christ Jesus] came and preached
peace to you who were far away
and peace to those who were near.*

Ephesians 2:17, NIV

Wherever [Jesus] went . . . they laid the sick in the marketplaces, and begged him that they might touch even the fringe of his cloak; and all who touched it were healed.

Mark 6:56, NRSV

The apostles gathered around Jesus, and told him all that they had done and taught. He said to them, "Come away to a deserted place by yourselves and rest a while."

Mark 6:31, NRSV

Never be content with the degree of love
you have for God. Seek to love God
more and more, and yet more. | Albert Edward Day

In [Christ Jesus] you . . . are
built together spiritually into
a dwelling place for God.
Ephesians 2:22, NRSV

2 Samuel 7:1-14*a*
Psalm 89:20-37
Ephesians 2:11-22
Mark 6:30-34, 53-56

MONDAY • JULY 21

"There is a boy here who has five barley loaves and two fish. But what are they among so many people." . . . about five thousand in all. Then Jesus took the loaves, and when he had given thanks, he distributed them to those who were seated; so also the fish, as much as they wanted.

John 6:9-11, NRSV

TUESDAY • JULY 22

I pray that . . . Christ may dwell in your hearts through faith, as you are being rooted and grounded in love.

Ephesians 3:16-17, NRSV

To him who is able to do immeasurably more than all we ask or imagine, according to his power at work within us, to him be glory . . . throughout all generations, for ever and ever! Amen.

Ephesians 3:20-21, NIV

Fools say in their hearts, "There is no God." They are corrupt, they do abominable deeds; there is no one who does good.

Psalm 14:1, NRSV

May you come to know [God's]
love—although it can never be
fully known—and be so
completely filled with the
very nature of God.

Ephesians 3:19, GNT

The Lord looks down from heaven
on humankind to see if there are
any who are wise, who seek
after God.

Psalm 14:2, NRSV

What better way to reveal God's love beyond our
works than to stop our usual works and discover that
Love is not withdrawn, but strongly visible for us? | Tilden Edwards

I pray that you may have the power to comprehend, with all the saints, what is the breadth and length and height and depth, and to know the love of Christ that surpasses knowledge, so that you may be filled with all the fullness of God.

Ephesians 4:18-19, NRSV

2 Samuel 11:1-15
Psalm 14
Ephesians 3:14-21
John 6:1-21

MONDAY • JULY 28

Sincerity and truth are what you require [O God]; fill my mind with your wisdom.

Psalm 51:6, GNT

TUESDAY • JULY 29

Each one of us has received a special gift in proportion to what Christ has given.

Ephesians 4:7, GNT

Restore to me the joy of your salvation and grant me a willing spirit, to sustain me.

Psalm 51:12, NIV

Nathan said to David, "Why did you despise the word of the LORD by doing what is evil in his eyes?"

2 Samuel 12:9, NIV

FRIDAY • AUGUST 1

Speaking the truth in love,
we will in all things grow up
into him who is the Head, that
is, Christ.

Ephesians 4:15, NIV

SATURDAY • AUGUST 2

Jesus said to [the crowd], "I am
the bread of life. Whoever comes
to me will never be hungry, and
whoever believes in me will never
be thirsty."

John 6:35, NRSV

We ourselves feel that what we are doing is just a drop in the ocean. But if that drop was not in the ocean, I think the ocean would be less because of that missing drop. I do not agree with the big way of doing things. To us what matters is an individual.

Mother Teresa
of Calcutta

*Lead a life worthy of the calling
to which you have been called,
with all humility and gentleness,
with patience, bearing with one
another in love, making every
effort to maintain the unity of the
Spirit in the bond of peace.*

Ephesians 4:1-3, NRSV

2 Samuel 11:26–12:13*a*
Psalm 51:1-12
Ephesians 4:1-16
John 6:24-35

MONDAY • AUGUST 4

Your ancestors ate manna in the desert, but they died. But the bread that comes down from heaven is of such a kind that whoever eats it will not die.

John 6:49-50, GNT

TUESDAY • AUGUST 5

Jesus said, *"I am the living bread that came down from heaven. If anyone eats this bread, he will live forever."*

John 6:51, GNT

WEDNESDAY • AUGUST 6

O Israel, put your hope in the
LORD, for with the LORD is
unfailing love and with him
is full redemption.

Psalm 130:7, NIV

THURSDAY • AUGUST 7

Putting away falsehood, let all
of us speak the truth to our
neighbors, for we are members
of one another.

Ephesians 4:25, NRSV

FRIDAY • AUGUST 8

*Put away from you all bitterness
and wrath and anger and
wrangling and slander, together
with all malice, and be kind to
one another, tenderhearted,
forgiving one another, as God
in Christ has forgiven you.*

Ephesians 4:31-32, NRSV

SATURDAY • AUGUST 9

*Let no evil talk come out of your
mouths, but only what is useful
for building up, as there is need,
so that your words may give grace
to those who hear.*

Ephesians 4:29, NRSV

Prayer leads you to see new paths and to hear new melodies in the air. Prayer is the breath of your life which gives you freedom to go and stay where you wish and to find the many signs which point out the way to a new land. Henri J. M. Nouwen

*Be imitators of God, as beloved
children, and live in love, as
Christ loved us.*
Ephesians 5:1-2a, NRSV

2 Samuel 18:5-9, 15, 31-33
Psalm 130
Ephesians 4:25–5:2
John 6:35, 41-51

MONDAY • AUGUST 11

*How wonderful are the things
the Lord does! All who are
delighted with them want to
understand them.*

Psalm 111:2, GNT

TUESDAY • AUGUST 12

*Be very careful, then, how you
live—not as unwise but as wise,
making the most of every
opportunity. . . . Therefore, do
not be foolish, but understand
what the Lord's will is.*

Ephesians 5:15-17, NIV

Jesus said to [the Jews], "Very truly, I tell you, unless you eat the flesh of the Son of Man and drink his blood, you have no life in you."

John 6:53, NRSV

All [the LORD] does is full of honor and majesty; his righteousness is eternal.

Psalm 111:3, GNT

FRIDAY • AUGUST 15

*[The LORD's] works are truth
and justice; his precepts all stand
on firm foundations, strongly
based to endure for ever, their
fabric goodness and truth.*

Psalm 111:7-8, NEB

SATURDAY • AUGUST 16

*The fear of the LORD is the
beginning of wisdom; all who
follow his precepts have good
understanding.*

Psalm 111:10, NIV

Where shall we sense the fragrance of obedience, if not in prayer? Where strip ourselves of the self-love that makes us impatient when insulted or made to suffer? Or put on a divine love that will make us patient, and ready to glory in the cross of Christ crucified? In prayer.

Catherine of Siena

Be filled with the Spirit, . . .
singing and making melody to
the Lord in your hearts, giving
thanks to God the Father at all
times and for everything in the
name of our Lord Jesus Christ.
Ephesians 5:18*b*-20, NRSV

1 Kings 2:10-12; 3:3-14
Psalm 111
Ephesians 5:15-20
John 6:51-58

Be strong in the Lord and in
the strength of his power.

Ephesians 6:10, NRSV

Solomon prayed, *"O LORD,*
God of Israel, there is no God like
you in heaven above or on
earth below—you who keep
your covenant of love with
your servants who continue
wholeheartedly in your way."

1 Kings 8:23, NIV

*I would rather stand at the gate
of the house of my God than live
in the homes of the wicked.*

Psalm 84:10, GNT

Jesus said, *"Just as the living
Father sent me and I live because
of the Father, so the one who feeds
on me will live because of me."*

John 6:57, NIV

*Our struggle is not against
enemies of blood and flesh, but
against the rulers, against the
authorities, against the cosmic
powers of this present darkness,
against the spiritual forces of evil
in the heavenly places.*

Ephesians 6:12, NRSV

Solomon prayed, *"Will God
really dwell on earth? The
heavens, even the highest heaven,
cannot contain you. How much
less this temple I have built!"*

1 Kings 8:27, NIV

Blessed be Thou, my Lord, for
the gift of all Thy creatures
and especially for our brother,
Master Sun, by whom the day
is enlightened. | Saint Francis of Assisi

Do all . . . in prayer, asking
for God's help. Pray on every
occasion as the Spirit leads. . . .
pray always for all God's people.
Ephesians 6:18, GNT

1 Kings 8:1, 6, 10-11, 22-30, 41-43
Psalm 84
Ephesians 6:10-20
John 6:56-69

MONDAY • AUGUST 25

Every generous act of giving,
with every perfect gift, is from
above, coming down from the
Father of lights, with whom there
is no variation or shadow due
to change.

James 1:17, NRSV

TUESDAY • AUGUST 26

Jesus said to the scribes and
Pharisees, "You abandon the
commandment of God and hold
to human tradition."

Mark 7:8, NRSV

*Everyone must be quick to listen,
but slow to speak, and slow to
become angry.*

James 1:19, GNT

*Away then with all that is sordid,
and the malice that hurries to
excess, and quietly accept the
message planted in your hearts,
which can bring you salvation.*

James 1:21, NEB

*There is nothing outside a person
that by going in can defile, but
the things that come out are
what defile.*

Mark 7:15, NRSV

*Be ye doers of the word, and
not hearers only, deceiving your
own selves.*

James 1:22, KJV

Breathe in the breath of the Spirit. Be free. Be simple. Prayer is a perfectly natural relationship between God, who loved you first, and you who try to love [God] back.

Catherine de Hueck Doherty

What God the Father considers to be pure and genuine religion is this: to take care of orphans and widows in their suffering and to keep oneself from being corrupted by the world.

James 1:27, GNT

Song of Solomon 2:8-13
Psalm 45:1-2, 6-9 *or* Psalm 72
James 1:17-27
Mark 7:1-8, 14-15, 21-23

MONDAY • SEPTEMBER 1

*Rich and poor have this in
common: the LORD is the Maker
of them all.*

Proverbs 22:2, NIV

TUESDAY • SEPTEMBER 2

*As the mountains surround
Jerusalem, so the LORD
surrounds his people both
now and forevermore.*

Psalm 125:2, NIV

WEDNESDAY • SEPTEMBER 3

As believers in our Lord Jesus Christ, you must never treat people in different ways according to their outward appearance.

James 2:1, GNT

THURSDAY • SEPTEMBER 4

Has not God chosen those who are poor in the eyes of the world to be rich in faith and to inherit the kingdom he promised those who love him?

James 2:5, NIV

FRIDAY • SEPTEMBER 5

*[The people in the crowd]were
astounded beyond measure,
saying, "He has done everything
well; he even makes the deaf to
hear and the mute to speak."*

Mark 7:37, NRSV

SATURDAY • SEPTEMBER 6

*So it is with faith: if it is alone
and includes no actions, then it
is dead.*

James 2:17, GNT

Each one of us is a temple of the Holy One. Each of us carries a spiritual power in us that can cause even the tiniest of faith-seeds to grow. It is vital that we protect and nurture this relationship so that it thrives.   Joyce Rupp

Suppose there are brothers or sisters who need clothes and don't have enough to eat. What good is there in your saying to them, "God bless you! Keep warm and eat well!"—if you don't give them the necessities of life?

James 2:15-16, GNT

Proverbs 22:1-2, 8-9, 22-23
Psalm 125 *or* Psalm 124
James 2:1-17
Mark 7:24-37

MONDAY • SEPTEMBER 8

Hold back thy servant . . . from sins of self-will, lest they get the better of me. Then I shall be blameless and innocent of any great transgression.

Psalm 19:13, NEB

TUESDAY • SEPTEMBER 9

From the same mouth come blessing and cursing. My brothers and sisters, this ought not to be so.

James 3:10, NRSV

"What about you?" [Jesus] asked [Peter]. "Who do you say that I am?"

Mark 8:29, NIV

The tongue is a small part of the body, but it makes great boasts. Consider what a great forest is set on fire by a small spark.

James 3:5, NIV

FRIDAY • SEPTEMBER 12

Jesus said, *"Those who are
ashamed of me and of my words
in this adulterous and sinful
generation, of them the Son of
Man will also be ashamed when
he comes in the glory of his Father
with the holy angels."*

Mark 8:38, NRSV

SATURDAY • SEPTEMBER 13

*The laws of the LORD are right,
and those who obey them are
happy.*

Psalm 19:8, GNT

Contemplation of Christ does not mean an emotional sort of pious daydream; it means entering by a deliberate, self-oblivious and humble attention into the tremendous mysteries of His Life—mysteries which each give us some deep truth about the Life and Will of God and the power and vocation of a soul that is given to God.

Evelyn Underhill

How clearly the sky reveals God's glory! How plainly it shows what he has done! Each day announces it to the following day; each night repeats it to the next.

Psalm 19:1-2, GNT

Proverbs 1:20-33
Psalm 19
James 3:1-12
Mark 8:27-38

*Who is wise and understanding
among you? Show by your good
life that your works are done with
gentleness born of wisdom.*

James 3:13, NRSV

*He sat down, called the twelve,
and said to them, "Whoever
wants to be first must be last of
all and servant of all."*

Mark 9:35, NRSV

Where there is jealousy and selfishness, there is also disorder and every kind of evil.

James 3:16, GNT

Taking [a little child] in his arms, [Jesus] said to [his disciples], "Whoever welcomes one such child in my name welcomes me, and whoever welcomes me welcomes not me but the one who sent me."

Mark 9:36-37, NRSV

FRIDAY • SEPTEMBER 19

*The wisdom that comes from
heaven is first of all pure;
then peace loving, considerate,
submissive, full of mercy and good
fruit, impartial and sincere.*

James 3:17, NIV

SATURDAY • SEPTEMBER 20

*Where do all the fights and
quarrels among you come from?
They come from your desires for
pleasure, which are constantly
fighting within you.*

James 4:1, GNT

[God's] love lies underneath
everything. We must grasp it as the
solid foundation of our religious life,
not growing up into that love, but
growing up out of it. Andrew Murray

Peacemakers who sow in peace
raise a harvest of righteousness.
James 3:18, NIV

Proverbs 31:10-31
Psalm 1
James 3:13–4:3, 7-8*a*
Mark 9:30-37

MONDAY • SEPTEMBER 22

Our help comes from the LORD,
who made heaven and earth.

Psalm 124:8, GNT

TUESDAY • SEPTEMBER 23

Jesus said, *"Whoever is not*
against us is for us."

Mark 9:40, NRSV

Are any among you suffering?
They should pray. Are any
cheerful? They should sing songs
of praise.
James 5:13, NRSV

The prayer of the righteous
is powerful and effective.
James 5:16b, NRSV

FRIDAY • SEPTEMBER 26

Confess your sins to one another,
and pray for one another, so that
you may be healed.

James 5:16*a*, NRSV

SATURDAY • SEPTEMBER 27

Jesus said, *". . . if salt has lost*
its saltiness, how can you season
it? Have salt in yourselves, and
be at peace with one another."

Mark 9:50, NRSV

God picks us up out of our everyday view of things only to set us down again for a little while so that we may see the world, the people around us, and even something of the mystery of God's self from the place of God's own compassionate vision.

Roberta C. Bondi

My friends, if any of you wander away from the truth and another one brings you back again, remember this: whoever turns a sinner back from the wrong way will save that sinner's soul from death and bring about the forgiveness of many sins.

James 5:19-20, GNT

Esther 7:1-6, 9-10; 9:20-22
Psalm 124
James 5:13-20
Mark 9:38-50

MONDAY • SEPTEMBER 29

Test me, O LORD, and try me,
examine my heart and my mind;
for your love is ever before me,
and I walk continually in
your truth.

Psalm 26:2-3, NIV

TUESDAY • SEPTEMBER 30

You have made [human beings]
for a little while lower than the
angels; you have crowned them
with glory and honor, subjecting
all things under their feet.

Hebrews 2:7-8, NRSV

[God's Son] reflects the brightness of God's glory and is the exact likeness of God's own being, sustaining the universe with his powerful word.

Hebrews 1:3, GNT

It was fitting that God, for whom and through whom all things exist, in bringing many children to glory, should make the pioneer of their salvation perfect through sufferings.

Hebrews 2:10, NRSV

Jesus said, *"I tell you the truth,*
anyone who will not receive the
kingdom of God like a little child
will never enter it."

Mark 10:15, NIV

I love the house where you live,
O LORD, the place where your
glory dwells.

Psalm 26:8, GNT

[Our lives] will be enriched by the gift of a listening ear—one who will pay attention to movements of grace and the tremors of change. Listening for the whispers of God is one of the most prized gifts we can offer each other.

Larry J. Peacock

*[Jesus] said to [his disciples],
"Let the little children come to
me, and do not hinder them, for
the kingdom of God belongs to
such as these."*

Mark 10:14, NIV

Job 1:1; 2:1-10
Psalm 26
Hebrews 1:1-4; 2:5-12
Mark 10:2-16

Job replied, "Even today my complaint is bitter. . . . If only I knew where to find him; if only I could go to his dwelling!"

Job 23:1-3, NIV

Indeed, the word of God is living and active, sharper than any two-edged sword . . . ; it is able to judge the thoughts and intentions of the heart.

Hebrews 4:12, NRSV

*My God, my God, why have
you abandoned me? I have cried
desperately for help, but still
it does not come.*

Psalm 22:1, GNT

*Before [God] no creature is
hidden, but all are naked and
laid bare to the eyes of the one to
whom we must render an account.*

Hebrews 4:13, NRSV

I have relied on you since the day
I was born, and you have always
been my God. Do not stay away
from me! Trouble is near, and
there is no one to help.

Psalm 22:10-11, GNT

Let us therefore approach the
throne of grace with boldness, so
that we may receive mercy and
find grace to help in time of need.

Hebrews 4:16, NRSV

Let me seek, then, the gift of silence, and poverty, and solitude, where everything I touch is turned into prayer: where the sky is my prayer, the birds are my prayer, the wind in the trees is my prayer, for God is all in all. Thomas Merton

Jesus said to the rich man, "You lack one thing; go, sell what you own, and give the money to the poor, and you will have treasure in heaven; then come, follow me."

Mark 10:21, NRSV

Job 23:1-9, 16-17
Psalm 22:1-15
Hebrews 4:12-16
Mark 10:17-31

Even the Son of Man did not come to be served, but to serve, and to give his life as a ransom for many.

Mark 10:45, NIV

The LORD answered Job out of the whirlwind: "Where were you when I laid the foundation of the earth? Tell me, if you have understanding."

Job 38:1, 4, NRSV

*You set the earth on its
foundations, so that it shall
never be shaken.*

Psalm 104:5, NRSV

*Bless the LORD, O my soul.
O LORD my God, thou art
very great; thou art clothed
with honour and majesty. [You]
coverest thyself in light as with
a garment.*

Psalm 104:1-2, KJV

Who has the wisdom to count the clouds? Who can tip over the water jars of the heavens when the dust becomes hard and the clods of earth stick together?

Job 38:37-38, NIV

Christ . . . did not take upon himself the glory of becoming a high priest. But God said to him, "You are my Son; today I have become your Father."

Hebrews 5:5, NIV

We find by losing. We
hold fast by letting go.
We become something
new by ceasing to be
something old. | Frederick Buechner

In his life on earth Jesus made his prayers and requests with loud cries and tears to God, who could save him from death. Because he was humble and devoted, God heard him. But even though he was God's Son, he learned through his sufferings to be obedient.

Hebrews 5:7-8, GNT

Job 38:1-7, 34-41
Psalm 104:1-9, 24, 35c
Hebrews 5:1-10
Mark 10:35-45

MONDAY • OCTOBER 20

*Job replied to the LORD: "I know
that you can do all things; no
plan of yours can be thwarted."*
Job 42:1-2, NIV

TUESDAY • OCTOBER 21

*Job replied to the LORD, "You
asked, 'Who is this that obscures
my counsel without knowledge?'
Surely I spoke of things I did not
understand, things too wonderful
for me to know."*
Job 42:1, 3, NIV

*My soul makes its boast in the
LORD; let the humble hear and
be glad.*

Psalm 34:2, NRSV

*Job replied to the LORD, "My
ears had heard of you but now
my eyes have seen you. Therefore
I despise myself and repent in
dust and ashes."*

Job 42:1, 5-6, NIV

*Find out for yourself how good the
LORD is. Happy are those who
find safety with him.*

Psalm 34:8, GNT

*Proclaim with me the LORD's
greatness; let us praise his name
together!*

Psalm 34:3, GNT

Everybody prays. People pray whether or not they call it prayer. We pray every time we ask for help, understanding, or strength, in or out of religion. Then, who and what we are speak out of us whether we know it or not. Ann and Barry Ulanov

Because Jesus lives forever, he has a permanent priesthood. Therefore he is able to save completely those who come to God through him, because he always lives to intercede for them.

Hebrews 7:24-25, NIV

Job 42:1-6, 10-17
Psalm 34:1-8, 19-22
Hebrews 7:23-28
Mark 10:46-52

MONDAY • OCTOBER 27

Do not put your trust in princes,
in mortals, in whom there is no
help. When their breath departs,
they return to the earth; on that
very day their plans perish.

Psalm 146:3-4, NRSV

TUESDAY • OCTOBER 28

"The most important
[commandment]," answered Jesus
[to a teacher of the law], "is this:
'Hear, O Israel, the Lord our
God, the Lord is one. Love the
Lord your God with all your
heart and with all your soul and
with all your mind and with all
your strength.'"

Mark 12:29-30, NIV

The second [commandment] is this: "Love your neighbor as yourself."

Mark 12:31, NIV

Happy are those . . . whose hope is in the Lord their God, who made heaven and earth, the sea, and all that is in them; who keeps faith forever.

Psalm 146:5-6, NRSV

*The LORD watches over the alien
and sustains the fatherless and
the widow, but he frustrates the
ways of the wicked.*

Psalm 146:9, NIV

*The blood of Christ, who through
the eternal Spirit offered himself
without blemish to God, [will]
purify our conscience from dead
works to worship the living God!*

Hebrews 9:14, NRSV

The spiritual quest is not retraced steps. It is venturing into new lands, along paths we have never walked, marked only by the footprints of those who have gone before us, and lighted by the invitation to "come follow me." John Kirvin

© International by Robert Cushman Hayes

*Ruth said, "Do not press me to
leave you or to turn back from
following you! Where you go, I
will go; where you lodge, I will
lodge; your people shall be my
people, and your God my God."*

Ruth 1:16, NRSV

Ruth 1:1-18
Psalm 146
Hebrews 9:11-14
Mark 12:28-34

*Christ did not enter a sanctuary
made by human hands, a mere
copy of the true one, but he
entered into heaven itself, now
to appear in the presence of God
on our behalf.*

Hebrews 9:24, NRSV

*If the LORD does not build the
house, the work of the builders
is useless.*

Psalm 127:1, GNT

[Christ] has appeared once and for all at the climax of history to abolish sins by the sacrifice of himself.

Hebrews 9:26, NEB

Why are you cast down, O my soul, and why are you disquieted within me? Hope in God; for I shall again praise him, my help and my God.

Psalm 42:11, NRSV

FRIDAY • NOVEMBER 7

I thirst for you, the living God.
When can I go and worship in
your presence?

Psalm 42:2, GNT

SATURDAY • NOVEMBER 8

As a deer longs for flowing
streams, so my soul longs for
you, O God.

Psalm 42:1, NRSV

God is a God of Love. Just as the sun cannot stop
shining so God cannot stop loving. And the whole
history of [hu]mankind is the history of
[humanity's] struggle to learn how to perceive and
return the Love that God bestows . . . so freely. | Toyohiko Kagawa

Jesus said, "I tell you the truth, this poor widow [who put in two very small copper coins] has put more into the treasury than all the others. They all gave out of their wealth; but she, out of her poverty, put in everything—all she had to live on."

Mark 12:43-44, NIV

Ruth 3:1-5; 4:13-17
Psalm 127 *or* Psalm 42
Hebrews 9:24-28
Mark 12:38-44

Hannah said, *"There is no Holy One like the LORD, no one besides you; there is no Rock like our God."*

1 Samuel 2:2, NRSV

Let us come near to God with a sincere heart and a sure faith, with hearts that have been purified from a guilty conscience and with bodies washed with clean water.

Hebrews 10:22, GNT

WEDNESDAY • NOVEMBER 12

From the rising of the sun to the place where it sets, the name of the LORD is be praised.
Psalm 113:3, NIV

THURSDAY • NOVEMBER 13

Where [sins and wicked deeds] have been forgiven, there are offerings for sins no longer.
Hebrews 10:18, NEB

FRIDAY • NOVEMBER 14

*Let us consider how to provoke
one another to love and good
deeds, not neglecting to meet
together, as is the habit of some,
but encouraging one another.*

Hebrews 10:24-25a, NRSV

SATURDAY • NOVEMBER 15

*The foundations of the earth
belong to the LORD; on them
he has built the world.*

1 Samuel 2:8, GNT

God has not promised a state of
constant bliss or a problem-free
existence but has promised to be
present in the silence and in the
dark, to exist alongside us,
within us, and for us. | Philip Yancey

*Let us hold unswervingly to
the hope we profess, for he
who promised is faithful.*

Hebrews 10:23, NIV

1 Samuel 1:4-20
1 Samuel 2:1-10 *or* Psalm 113
Hebrews 10:11-25
Mark 13:1-8

*One who rules over people justly,
ruling in the fear of God, is like
the light of morning, like the sun
rising on a cloudless morning,
gleaming from the rain on the
grassy land.*

2 Samuel 23:3-4, NRSV

*"I am the Alpha and the
Omega," says the Lord God,
"who is, and who was, and who
is to come, the Almighty."*

Revelation 1:8, NIV

[Jesus Christ] loves us, and by his sacrificial death he has freed us from our sins and made us a kingdom of priests to serve his God and Father.

Revelation 1:5-6, GNT

Look, he is coming with the clouds, and every eye will see him, even those who pierced him; and all the peoples of the earth will mourn because of him. So shall it be! Amen.

Revelation 1:7, NIV

Jesus said, "My kingdom is not of this world. If it were, my servants would fight to prevent my arrest by the Jews. But now my kingdom is from another place."

John 18:36, NIV

To Jesus Christ be the glory and power forever and ever! Amen.

Revelation 1:6, GNT

. . . every tree is known by its own fruit, and love too is known by its fruit, and the love about which Christianity speaks is known by its own fruit because it has the truth of the eternal in it. | Søren Kierkegaard

CHRIST THE KING SUNDAY

Jesus answered [Pilate], "You are right in saying I am a king. In fact, for this reason I was born, and for this I came into the world, to testify to the truth. Everyone on the side of truth listens to me."

John 18:37, NIV

2 Samuel 23:1-7
Psalm 132:1-12
John 18:33-37
Revelation 1:4b-8

"The days are coming," declares the LORD, "when I will fulfill the gracious promise I made to the house of Israel and to the house of Judah."

Jeremiah 33:14, NIV

Teach me to live according to your truth, for you are my God, who saves me. I always trust in you.

Psalm 25:5, GNT

Good and upright is the LORD;
therefore he instructs sinners in
the way. He leads the humble
in what is right, and teaches
the humble his way.

Psalm 25:8-9, NRSV

Jesus said, *"Heaven and earth*
will pass away, but my words
will never pass away."

Luke 21:33, GNT

*The LORD said, "In those days,
and at that time, will I cause the
Branch of righteousness to grow
up unto David; and he shall
execute judgment and
righteousness in the land."*

Jeremiah 33:15, KJV

*Be on guard so that your hearts
are not weighed down with
dissipation and drunkenness and
the worries of this life, and [the
coming of the Son of Man] catch
you unexpectedly, like a trap. For
it will come upon all who live on
the face of the whole earth.*

Luke 21:34-35, NRSV

The most important preparation for Christmas is one that will not go on a wall, a door, a table, or under the tree. The most important preparation for Christmas is still the building of the road through the desert, the preparation in our spiritually barren world of a way for the Lord to walk. Mary Anna Vidakovich

FIRST SUNDAY OF ADVENT

Make me to know your ways,
O LORD; teach me your paths.

Psalm 25:1-10, NRSV

Jeremiah 33:14-16
Psalm 25:1-10
1 Thessalonians 3:9-13
Luke 21:25-36

MONDAY • DECEMBER 1

Zechariah said, *"Let us praise the Lord, the God of Israel! He has come to the help of his people and has set them free."*

Luke 1:68, GNT

TUESDAY • DECEMBER 2

"See, I will send my messenger, who will prepare the way before me. Then suddenly the LORD you are seeking will come to his temple; the messenger of the covenant, whom you desire, will come," says the LORD Almighty.

Malachi 3:1, NIV

Who can endure the day of his coming? Who can stand when [the LORD's messenger] appears? For he will be like a refiner's fire or a launderer's soap.

Malachi 3:2, NIV

Zechariah said, *"By the tender mercy of our God, the dawn from on high will break upon us, to give light to those who sit in darkness and in the shadow of death, to guide our feet into the way of peace."*

Luke 1:78-79, NRSV

FRIDAY • DECEMBER 5

Paul wrote, *"I am sure that God, who began this good work in you, will carry it on until it is finished on the Day of Christ Jesus."*

Philippians 1:6, GNT

SATURDAY • DECEMBER 6

Paul wrote, *"I pray that your love will keep on growing more and more, together with true knowledge and perfect judgment, so that you will be able to choose what is best."*

Philippians 1:9-10, GNT

Love is a fruit in season at all times, and within reach of every hand. Anyone may gather it and no limit is set. Everyone can reach this love through meditation, spirit of prayer, and sacrifice, by an intense inner life.

Mother Teresa
of Calcutta

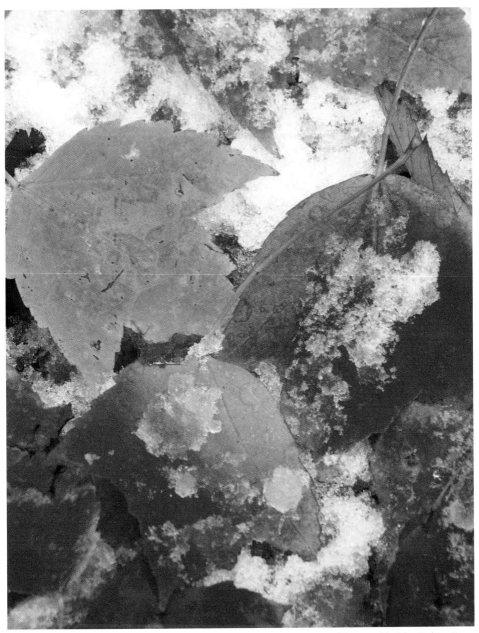

SECOND SUNDAY OF ADVENT

Prepare the way of the Lord, make his paths straight. Every valley shall be filled, and every mountain and hill shall be made low, and the crooked shall be made straight, and the rough ways made smooth; and all flesh shall see the salvation of God.

Luke 3:4-6, NRSV

Malachi 3:1-4
Luke 1:68-79
Philippians 1:3-11
Luke 3:1-6

The LORD said, ". . . I will deal
with all who oppressed you; I will
rescue the lame and gather those
who have been scattered. . . . At
that time I will gather you; at
that time I will bring you home."

Zephaniah 3:19-20, NIV

Surely God is my salvation; I
will trust, and will not be afraid,
for the LORD God is my strength
and my might; he has become
my salvation.

Isaiah 12:2, NRSV

*Whoever has two coats must
share with anyone who has none;
and whoever has food must do
likewise.*

Luke 3:11, NRSV

Paul wrote, *"May you always be
joyful in your union with the
Lord. I say it again: rejoice!"*

Philippians 4:4, GNT

John said, *"I baptize you with water; but one who is more powerful than I is coming; I am not worthy to untie the thong of his sandals. He will baptize you with the Holy Spirit and fire."*

Luke 3:16, NRSV

Let your gentleness be evident to all. The Lord is near.

Philippians 4:5, NIV

When angels begin to sing we should look for the world to be turned upside down. Angels never come to proclaim the everyday, only the extraordinary.

Mary Anna Vidakovich

THIRD SUNDAY OF ADVENT

Do not be anxious about anything, but in everything, by prayer and petition, with thanksgiving, present your requests to God. And the peace of God, which transcends all understanding, will guard your hearts and your minds in Christ Jesus.
Philippians 4:6-7, NIV

Zephaniah 3:14-20
Isaiah 12:2-6
Philippians 4:4-7
Luke 3:7-18

Mary said, "My soul magnifies the Lord, and my spirit rejoices in God my Savior . . . for the Mighty One has done great things for me, and holy is his name."

Luke 1:47, 49, NRSV

The LORD said, "You, Bethlehem Ephrathah, though you are small among the clans of Judah, out of you will come for me one who will be ruler over Israel, whose origins are from of old, from ancient times."

Micah 5:2, NIV

When Elizabeth heard Mary's
greeting, the baby moved within
her. Elizabeth was filled with the
Holy Spirit and said in a loud
voice, "You are the most blessed
of all women, and blessed is the
child you will bear!"

Luke 1:41-42, GNT

[The one who will come for the
LORD] will stand and shepherd
his flock in the strength of
the Lord . . . and he will be
their peace.

Micah 5:4-5, NIV

Elizabeth said to Mary,
*"Blessed is she who believed
that there would be a fulfillment
of what was spoken to her by
the Lord."*

Luke 1:45, NRSV

*[The Lord's] mercy is for those
who fear him from generation
to generation. He has shown
strength with his arm; he
has scattered the proud in the
thoughts of their hearts. . . .
he has filled the hungry with
good things, and sent the rich
away empty.*

Luke 1:50-53, NRSV

One does not adequately prepare for the coming of Christmas merely by unpacking the attic boxes marked "decorations" in time for the tree and the company, only to be put away again until next December. Advent's preparations initiate ongoing disciplines to make room for the coming of Christ into our lives, our communities, and our churches. We make room for God's holy presence by sweeping out the unholy through the discipline of confession and repentance. We make room for Christ's incarnation among us by remembering that how we treat one another reflects how we treat our Lord. Faithfulness to Advent's disciplined preparation comes in welcoming the very dwelling of God within us. | John Indermark

FOURTH SUNDAY OF ADVENT

When Christ was about to come into the world, he said to God: ". . . you have prepared a body for me. . . . Here I am, to do your will, O God . . ."

Hebrews 10:5-7, GNT

Micah 5:2-5a
Luke 1:47-55
Hebrews 10:5-10
Luke 1:39-45

Praise the LORD. Praise the LORD from the heavens, praise him in the heights above. . . . for his name alone is exalted; his splendor is above the earth and the heavens.

Psalm 148:1, 13, NIV

Be forbearing with one another, and forgiving, where any of you has cause for complaint: you must forgive as the Lord forgave you.

Colossians 3:13, NEB

Whatever you do, in word or deed, do everything in the name of the Lord Jesus, giving thanks to God the Father through him.

Colossians 3:17, NRSV

CHRISTMAS DAY

The angel said to [the shepherds], "Do not be afraid; for see—I am bringing you good news of great joy for all the people: to you is born this day in the city of David a Savior, who is the Messiah, the Lord."

Luke 2:10-11, NRSV

On the third day they found
[Jesus] in the Temple, sitting with
the Jewish teachers, listening to
them and asking questions. All
who heard him were amazed at
his intelligent answers.

Luke 2:46-47, GNT

[Jesus] said to [his parents],
"Why were you searching for me?
Did you not know that I must be
in my Father's house?"

Luke 2:49, NRSV

God is a God of fresh beginnings. Of dawn. Of new life. Of a transfigured world where the most poignant language lodged in the human heart will be fulfilled. | Wendy M. Wright

As God's chosen people, holy and dearly loved, clothe yourselves with compassion, kindness, humility, gentleness and patience.

Colossians 3:12, NIV

1 Samuel 2:18-20, 26
Psalm 148
Colossians 3:12-17
Luke 2:1-20; 2:41-52

*Blessed be the God and Father of
our Lord Jesus Christ, who has
blessed us in Christ with every
spiritual blessing in the heavenly
places, just as he chose us in
Christ before the foundation
of the world to be holy and
blameless before him in love.*

Ephesians 1:3-4, NRSV

*In the beginning was the Word,
and the Word was with God,
and the Word was God.*

John 1:1, NRSV

*And the Word became flesh and
lived among us, and we have seen
his glory, the glory of the father's
only son, full of grace and truth.*

John 1:14, NRSV

ACKNOWLEDGMENTS

December 2002

Madame Guyon, *A Method of Prayer,* trans. Dugold MacFadyen (London: James Clark & Co., 1902), 110.

January 2003

Henry Van Dyke, *The Spirit of Christmas* (New York: Charles Scribner's Sons, 1905), 48.

Maxie Dunnam, *Let Me Say That Again* (Nashville, Tenn.: Upper Room Books, 1996), unpaged.

Henri J. M. Nouwen, *The Way of the Heart: Desert Spirituality and Contemporary Ministry* (New York: The Seabury Press, 1981), 30.

Kallistos Ware, *The Orthodox Way* (Crestwood, N.Y.: St. Vladimir's Seminary Press, 1980), 23.

February

Kathleen Fischer, *Winter Grace: Spirituality and Aging* (Nashville, Tenn.: Upper Room Books, 1998), 18.

Maria Boulding, *The Coming of God* (Collegeville, Minn.: The Liturgical Press, 1982), 2.

Howard Thurman, *Meditations of the Heart* (New York: Harper & Brothers, 1953), 49.

Kenneth L. Gibble, *Once Upon a Wonder: Imaginings from the Gospels* (Nashville, Tenn.: Upper Room Books, 1992), 39.

March

Evelyn Underhill, *Light of Christ* (London: Longmans, Green and Co., 1944), 41–42.

Renita J. Weems, *Listening for God: A Minister's Journey Through Silence and Doubt* (New York: Simon & Schuster, 1999), 120.

Thomas à Kempis, *The Imitation of Christ,* trans. Richard Whitford and ed. Harold C. Gardiner (New York: Doubleday, Image Book, 1955), 65.

Bonnie Thurston, *To Everything a Season: A Spirituality of Time* (New York: Crossroad Publishing Co., 1999), 109.

Joan Chittister, *Wisdom Distilled from the Daily: Living the Rule of St. Benedict Today* (New York: Harper & Row, 1990), 10.

April

John Sanford, *The Kingdom Within,* rev. ed. (New York: HarperCollins Publishers, 1987), 144.

Kevin Scully, *Sensing the Passion: Reflections during Lent* (Nashville, Tenn.: Upper Room Books, 2000), 138.

Barbara Brown Taylor, *Home by Another Way* (Boston, Mass.: Cowley Publications, 1999), 111–12.

The Rule of St. John the Evangelist (Cambridge, Mass.: Cowley Publications, 1997), 8.

May

Andrew Murray, *Andrew Murray on Prayer* (New Kensington, Penn.: Whitaker House, 1998), 339.

Kallistos Ware, *The Orthodox Way* (Crestwood, N.Y.: St. Vladimir's Seminary Press, 1980), 111.

Hannah Whitall Smith, *The Christian's Secret of a Happy Life* (Chicago: Fleming H. Revell, 1883), 184.

Augustine of Hippo, *The Confessions of Saint Augustine* (New York: Boni & Liveright, 1927), Book 10, 6:224.

June

Donald E. Demaray, editor and compiler, *Devotions and Prayers of Charles H. Spurgeon* (Grand Rapids, Mich.: Baker Book House, 1960), 92.

Baron Friedrich von Hügel, *The Life of Prayer* (New York: E. P. Dutton & Co., 1927), 16.

Eugene H. Peterson, *Working the Angles: The Shape of Pastoral Integrity* (Grand Rapids, Mich.: William B. Eerdmans, 1987), 43–44.

Saint Teresa of Avila, *Interior Castle*, ed. and trans. E. Allison Peers (New York: Doubleday, Image Book, 1961), 34.

Sue Bender, *Everyday Sacred: A Woman's Journey Home* (San Francisco: HarperSanFrancisco, 1995), 159.

July

Kallistos Ware, *The Orthodox Way* (Crestwood, N.Y.: St. Vladimir's Seminary Press, 1980), 16.

Catherine de Hueck Doherty, *Sobornost* (Notre Dame, Ind.: Ave Maria Press, 1977), 73.

Albert Edward Day, *Discipline and Discovery: The Revised Workbook Edition* (Nashville, Tenn.: The Upper Room, 1987), 120.

Tilden Edwards, *Sabbath Time: Understanding and Practice for Contemporary Christians* (Nashville, Tenn.: Upper Room Books, 1992), 91.

August

Mother Teresa of Calcutta, *A Gift for God: Prayers and Meditations* (San Francisco: Harper & Row, 1975), 40.

Henri J. M. Nouwen, *With Open Hands* (Notre Dame: Ind.: Ave Maria Press, 1972), 157.

Catherine of Siena, a 1379 letter in *A Life of Total Prayer: Selected Writings of Catherine of Siena*, ed. Keith Beasley-Topliffe (Nashville, Tenn.: Upper Room Books, 2000), 34.

Saint Francis of Assisi, *The Writings of St. Francis of Assisi*, trans. Constance, Countess de la Warr (London: Burns & Oates, [1905]), 118.

Catherine de Hueck Doherty, *Soul of My Soul* (Notre Dame, Ind.: Ave Maria Press, 1985), 113.

September

Joyce Rupp, *The Cup of Our Life: A Guide for Spiritual Growth* (Notre Dame, Ind.: Ave Maria Press, 1997), 22.

Evelyn Underhill, *Light of Christ* (London: Longmans, Green and Co., 1944), 27.

Andrew Murray, *Andrew Murray on Prayer* (New Kensington, Penn.: Whitaker House, 1998), 342.

Roberta C. Bondi, *Night on the Flint River: An Accidental Journey in Knowing God* (Nashville, Tenn.: Abingdon Press, 1999), 36–37.

October

Larry J. Peacock, *Heart and Soul* (Nashville, Tenn.: Upper Room Books, 1992), 24.

Thomas Merton, *Thoughts in Solitude* (New York: Farrar, Straus and Giroux, 1958), 94.

Frederick Buechner, *A Room Called Remember* (San Francisco: Harper & Row, 1984), 189.

Ann and Barry Ulanov, *Primary Speech: A Psychology of Prayer* (Atlanta: John Knox Press, 1982), 1.

November

John Kirvin, *God Hunger: Discovering the Mystic in All of Us* (Notre Dame, Ind.: Sorin Books, 1999), 52.

Toyohiko Kagawa, *Love: The Law of Life* (St. Paul, Minn.: Macalester Park Publishing Company, 1951), 27.

Philip Yancey, *Reaching for the Invisible God: What Can We Expect to Find?* (Grand Rapids, Mich.: Zondervan Publishing House, 2000), 181.

Søren Kierkegaard, *Works of Love*, trans. David F. Swenson and Lillian Marvin Swenson (Princeton, N.J.: Princeton University Press, 1946), 7.

Mary Anna Vidakovich, *Sing to the Lord: Devotions for Advent* (Nashville, Tenn.: Upper Room Books, 1994), 70.

December

Mother Teresa of Calcutta, *A Gift for God: Prayers and Meditations* (San Francisco: Harper & Row, 1975), 67.

Mary Anna Vidakovich, *Sing to the Lord: Devotions for Advent* (Nashville, Tenn.: Upper Room Books, 1994), 34.

John Indermark, *Setting the Christmas Stage: Readings for the Advent Season* (Nashville, Tenn.: Upper Room Books, 2001), 19.

Wendy M. Wright, *The Time Between: Cycles and Rhythms in Ordinary Time* (Nashville, Tenn.: Upper Room Books, 1999), 34.